THE TEENAGER'S GUIDE TO LIFE, THE UNIVERSE & BEING AWESOME

D1048720

THE TEENAGER'S GUIDE TO LIFE, THE UNIVERSE & BEING AWESOME

......

ANDY COPE (WITH
JASON TODD, ANDY WHITTAKER
& DARRELL WOODMAN)

First published in Great Britain in 2019 by Hodder and Stoughton.
An Hachette UK company.

This edition published in 2019 by John Murray Learning

British Library Cataloguing in Publication Data: a catalogue record for this title is available from the British Library.

Library of Congress Catalog Card Number: on file.

ISBN 978 1 473 67942 9

eISBN 978 1 473 67943 6

1

The publisher has used its best endeavours to ensure that any website addresses referred to in this book are correct and active at the time of going to press. However, the publisher and the author have no responsibility for the websites and can make no guarantee that a site will remain live or that the content will remain relevant, decent or appropriate.

The publisher has made every effort to mark as such all words which it believes to be trademarks. The publisher should also like to make it clear that the presence of a word in the book, whether marked or unmarked, in no way affects its legal status as a trademark.

Every reasonable effort has been made by the publisher to trace the copyright holders of material in this book. Any errors or omissions should be notified in writing to the publisher, who will endeavour to rectify the situation for any reprints and future editions.

Typeset by Integra Software Services Pvt. Ltd.

Printed and bound in Great Britain by Clays Ltd, Elcograf S.p.A.

John Murray Learning policy is to use papers that are natural, renewable and recyclable products and made from wood grown in sustainable forests. The logging and manufacturing processes are expected to conform to the environmental regulations of the country of origin.

Carmelite House
50 Victoria Embankment
London EC4Y 0DZ

www.hodder.co.uk

DEDICATION

For Scrump and Bwana. Thanks for making me so proud x

•••••••

CONTENTS

YOUR CONTRACT

This book comes with a contract. When you get older you'll realize that every contract comes with small print. Here's ours. Read it carefully now:

Para 1. Clause A1: I do solemnly swear to read this book, cover to cover, within the next two weeks. No, I haven't really got time but, hey, that's just a lazy excuse. I mean, I've got time for social media, games consoles, watching cat videos and practising my selfie so for the next fortnight, I'll do a little less of those things and a bit more reading.

Para 1. Clause A2: Oh, and writing. I also solemnly swear to complete the activities to the best of my ability. I will actually stop and think about what the authors are asking. Even when it gets difficult. In fact, especially when it gets difficult. [Addendum: Which it will. Quite often].

Para 2. Clause B1: I also promise no rolling of my eyes or tutting while reading this book and if the person who bought if for me asks how I'm getting on, I promise to smile, make eye contact and say it's utterly awesome.

Para 2. Clause B2: And I will also tell my mates it's awesome. Even if they don't ask.

Para 2. Clause B3: But on no account will I lend them mine. They need to buy their own copy. Otherwise how will the authors of said book ever get rich?

Para 3. Clause C1: Moreover, I hereby abide by the contract of 'action'. I understand that the information in this book is awesome, but that it cannot make me awesome unless I apply it. Once again, I understand that the application of said principles requires effort and practice. (See Para 3. Subsection i)

Para 3. Subsection i: From now on I will change the long heralded saying that 'practice makes perfect' because it pretty much doesn't. Well it sort of does, but I hereby declare that from this day forward, in sickness and in health, for richer or poorer, practice makes permanent. (See Para 3. Subsection ii)

Para 3. Subsection ii: Till death do I part. Or something like that?

Para 4. Clause D1: Anyhow, the long and short of it is that I get this book isn't actually a book. Well, obviously it is. But it isn't just a book. It's an opportunity. And the longer I leave it unopened, the shorter my life is becoming. I 'get' that if I read 'Awesome Teenager' it will enhance my mind, my thinking and my habits. It will, in actual fact, change my life. (See Para 4. Subsection iii)

Para 4. Subsection iii: We operate a no refunds policy. No book can, in fact, change your life. Only one 'thing' can change your life ['thing' – person or persons who can be bothered to take action specified in these pages. See Para 3 C1 & Subsection i]

Para 5. Clause E1: Someone once said why put off today what you can do a week on Tuesday. So I'm going to get cracking by signing this contract. Right now:

Name:

Date:

Signature:

Robot Test. We need to make sure you're a real person.
Please write the numbers and letters in the box below:

NomoreExCu5es

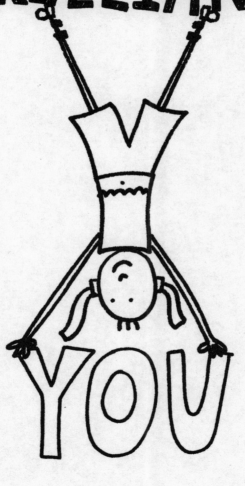

Part 1

BRILLIANT

YOU

BRILLIANT YOU

Welcome to the pleasure dome, our opening section that starts with numbers and then moves rapidly onto sea squirts, hitchhikers and why it's not always a great idea to take adult advice.

We find out about Andy's new toaster and his alien child, we learn how to get Aunty Janet to ask a better question and then, BOOM, we're into the science bit. Don't worry, it's not normal science, it's easy peasy science, and is backed up by a magnificent tale of the extra special Olympics.

Then it's back to the future and we explain why it's never a good idea for bus drivers to do brain surgery or, indeed, for brain surgeons to drive buses.

We introduce the 90:10 principle and a wobbly Jenga diagram in which we challenge you to raise your game. And, btw, have you ever considered what 'success' actually means? Not to anyone else, but to you?

Cos that's kind of where we're going in Part 1.

Confused? We certainly hope so. Strap yourself in – it's gonna get bumpy...

The Numbers Game

IMPORTANT NUMBERS

9: Number of lives, if you're a cat

43252003274489856000: the total number of configurations on a Rubik's cube

101: The room in which George Orwell put his worst nightmares

7: The world's favourite lucky number

13: Not so lucky

10: Commandments. Decent rules to live by. *'Thou shall not kill'* is a good one to bear in mind if you're planning on staying out of prison

70: the percentage increase in teenage anxiety and depression in the last two decades

75 million: The number of anti-depressants prescribed in the UK per annum (that's more than there are actual people)

One-seventh: The proportion of your life that is spent on Mondays – too many to wish away

15: There are 15 people who form the core of your life. These relationships will nourish and sustain you. So over-invest your time in the 15. You can be a failure on social media but hugely happy if you have a close-knit 15.

666: The number of the beast

**10,000,000,000,000,000,000,000,000,000,000,000,
000,000,000,000,000,000,000,000,000,000,000,
000,000,000,000,000,000,000,000,000,000,000:**
Googol. Often shortened to 10^{100}. Also known as ten
duotrigintillion or ten thousand sexdecillion

18: Almost but not quite grown up. Ditto 21

4,000: The number of weeks in the average UK lifespan

Number 1: Someone you should really look after

Welcome to the literary equivalent of 'ctrl/alt/delete'. All you
have to do is read the book, keep an open mind, scribble in
the appropriate spaces, and apply the learning. Then, as if by
magic, you will re-boot with new mental software installed,
upgrading you to *'best possible self'*.

It's a very simple process that also happens to be *not very
easy*. Because, of course, if awesomeness was easy, everybody would be doing it. Look around you. What do you see?

Sea squirts, that's what. Bear with me ...

Get this, it's an actual fact, the humble sea squirt paddles
around until it finds a rock, attaches itself, gets comfy and
then eats its own brain. Its brain is useful in finding something to attach to but, once that bit's done, it doesn't need its
brain anymore so it scoffs it, thus providing a bit of suste-
nance so it can hang on for dear life.

I think there might be a human equivalent, people who
have settled on their rock, being bombarded by life, and

who stay put. Even though there might be a better rock, a bit higher where the sun makes life more pleasant and the waves are less intense. But, metaphorically, they've eaten their brains.

Let's go back to the numbers above, particularly the last couple. This book is about investing in number 1, to ensure that you have a cracking life. Remember, 4000 weeks is the *average* life-span. You might get a few more, or a few less, but there's a fair-to-middling chance that you'll be knocking about for around 4000 weeks.

Without us meddling in your life, it could be that you figure everything out on your own and end up acing school, meeting and marrying your perfect partner, having a stellar career, three wonderful kids, a holiday home in Florida and a fabulous 4000 weeks. In which case, we applaud you. If, on the other hand, you need the cheat codes, then this book will race you through a few levels, beating some end-of-level bosses along the way.

Fitting in is so last millennium. We can't think of a single human being who has ever achieved greatness by fitting in? And by 'greatness' we don't mean you have to try and be like Mother Teresa or Nelson Mandela. We mean daring to stand out, because that's where life gets really interesting. Suffice to say that in the limited time you have, we want you to make a dent in the universe.

So, in a book crammed with top tips and pithy advice, our first gem of wisdom is to quit comparing yourself to other people, and start matching yourself up against your own potential. It's a simple question: *Are you better today than you were yesterday?* If you can tick that particular box – *consistently* – you'll be growing. Not just a bit older, but a little bit wiser, every day

You are already the best in the world at being you. This book will help you get even better.

A MODERN PRAYER

Dear God

So far today I've done alright. I haven't gossiped. I haven't lost my temper. I haven't been greedy, moody, nasty or selfish. And I'm really glad about that. But in a few minutes, God, I'm going to get out of bed and from then on I'm going to need a lot more help. Thank you.

Amen

We are all born with magic inside us. We are whirlwinds of energy and learning. But we get the magic educated right out of us. We get it washed out, ironed out, smartened out, relationshipped out, ruled out and we learn to conform. We're told to grow up; be responsible and colour between the lines. The magic gets hidden. We forget. We're like Harry Potter, when he's lost his wand. Just another average speccy kid.

And why are we told to be responsible? Here's something that's harsh but true; because the people doing the telling are grown-ups who are ashamed that they've allowed their magic to wither in themselves.

'Average Speccy KID

Here's the problem with adults; they dish out a lot of advice that might or might not have worked for them, back in the day. Our argument is that those days are gone. *Your* days are different – radically faster, more pressurized and full-on than whenever 'back in the day' was. So some of the olde worlde advice is a bit cliched, such as *'live every day as if it's your last'*. Really? In a hospital bed surrounded by teary relatives?

We're not keen on that.

The other misleading cliché is that *'you only live once'*. Again, *really?* There are two in yer face problems with that. Firstly, it's often dished out to you by adults who are living a very mediocre life themselves and, secondly, is it even true? Or is it that you only *die* once? And that you live every single day?

This book is for right here, right now. New thinking for new times. We're going to go head to head against conventional wisdom and challenge you to do everything a bit better than you have to. That means being kinder than you have to, working harder than you have to, being more polite than you have to, listening better than you have to, doing your homework a bit better than you have to ...

Over time, all these tiny changes build up to a whopper of a difference. While everyone else is doing 'just enough' your 'do it better than I have to' mantra means you will power ahead.

I was late to catch on to the wondrous realization that everywhere I go, I'm there. So I can be queueing at the supermarket and I'll suddenly realize, *'Oh my gosh, I'm in a queue at the supermarket'*, or I can be at home and I'm like, *'I'm standing in my kitchen'*. The point being, I cannot escape from me. I'm stuck with myself for 4000 weeks. I can run as fast as I like, but I'm still stuck with me.

And you cannot escape from you. Not for a single second.

So I'm thinking, if I'm stuck with me for 4000 weeks, it makes sense to be stuck with a version of me that I'm proud of. A 'me' that's upbeat, positive, buzzing and confident, rather than the bog-standard me that I used to be. It took me about a third of my 4000 weeks to get it. We're hoping this book will help you get it a lot sooner.

Back to the numbers game that we opened with. Nine lives would be cool, but you ain't no pussy cat. The bare-knuckled truth? Your potential is one thing. What you do with it is quite another.

YOU ain't NO pussy cat

The Truth is Out There

INTERESTING THOUGHT

It's no good having your eyes wide open, if your mind is half-closed.

Before the off, we're going to make some assumptions.

First up, you didn't buy this book. Someone bought it for you and this 'someone' loves you dearly. They want you to have a brilliant life and the chances are you are already awesome. *Sometimes!* Saturdays maybe? They want you to learn to be awesome on a more permanent basis.

Second, *them* wanting you to have a brilliant life is not enough. *You* have to want it too.

And third, we're crediting you with enough nous to read this book, cover to cover. While your mates are Instagramming pictures of their lunch, you are tucking into these chapters, having a go at the activities, keeping an open mind and building your knowledge. We have very high expectations and we know that you can reach them.

So what exactly is this book? In short, it's designed to change your life. If that's too bold, let's downgrade to giving you a leg up to being a better version of yourself (which will, by spooky coincidence, change your life).

This book contains the truth, and nothing but the truth, or at least, our version of it. Which might not actually be true? We are also dead keen to provide some clarity, which might not be so clear and some wisdom that might not be so wise. And while we're on a roll, we might also provide some humour that isn't very humorous.

Because what is 'true', 'clear', 'wise' and 'funny' will depend on what's whizzing around your head.

But what *exactly* is the truth?

Scientists reckon the Earth's been around for about 14 billion years (give or take) and humans for 200,000 years. Both of those facts are true, or not, according to who you talk to.

Remember when the world was flat? Of course you don't, and it never was flat, but that's what everyone thought at the time. Pancake earth was the truth. Everyone, even the brightest minds on the planet, thought so. In fact they knew so. *'Don't sail too close to the horizon otherwise you'll fall off the end and die'* kind of focuses the mind. So people stayed put.

Then the rules changed. Someone found out the truth wasn't actually true – the world was round – so off they went discovering new worlds (slaughtering the locals who'd already discovered them might be closer to what actually happened).

For 199,000 of our *Homo sapien* years humanity inched along. They didn't have school, Netflix, YouTube or America. They definitely didn't have Wi-Fi or iPads, otherwise they'd have been able to Google *'Is the world actually flat?'* and chuckle at their foolishness.

For ever [*and ever and ever and ever*], humans have died from scarcity. Not enough food, clean water, sanitation, medication, warmth, safety ... and then WHAM, you were born and it all kicked off.

Congratulations! Here you are, the first generation in human history to be dying from too much!

Yes, in a bizarre twist of evolution, obesity is killing more people than starvation.

Of course, you don't know any different. You just crack on with your life, assuming the world's always been full of stuff. Everyone's always been eating till it hurts. People have always had 500 different types of trainers to choose from. That children have always gone to nice schools. That all people live in centrally-heated houses, have cars with cup holders and secret sunglasses compartments. And that Wi-Fi and smartphones have been around forever.

You are a social experiment, the first generation in the history of the world to be born scrolling, swiping and jabbing at screens.

You are born into a world that's new and different. Its super-fastness is super-exciting and for the next 50 years your world is going to accelerate to a cheek wobbling warp speed. The truth will be new. The rules new. Your thinking needs to be new too.

Which is where we stumble. The problem with human beings is that the pace of change has accelerated away but our brains and bodies continue to evolve slooooowly. The Lamborghini of change has left us in a dust storm.

This book will help you play catch-up.

The Secret

There's no doubt that school is important. It's a chance to invest in your future. All that reading, writing, trigonometry, war poetry and stuff. Lap it up. Enjoy it. It's useful in pub quizzes.

This book isn't about any of that. Think of it as an *un*-textbook.

Because one day you'll get a job interview for your dream career, like an atom splitter, quark engineer, Botox bottom engineer, FaceTube sales rep, or holiday imagineerer. And do you know what they *won't* ask? They *won't* ask you any of these:

- Can you please tell me about top heavy fractions
- How do you spell accommodation?
- Explain cell division and photosynthesis
- Any idea what an adjective is?
- Explain the basic plot of *Macbeth* or *Of Mice and Men*

So if that's exactly what they're *not* going to ask, what on earth will they want to know?

Here's your advance warning – to nail that dream job they'll ask you to talk about yourself. What kind of person are you? What qualities do you possess? Give examples of when you've been stand-out epic and inspired yourself and those around you. When have you been a hero? How do you deal with a crisis (and please give examples from real life).

Of course, it helps if you also know about fractions, photosynthesis, adjectives and *Macbeth*. It's really cool to be able to spell 'accommodation', especially if you're in the holiday imagineering business.

We're going to prep you for that dream job and that awesome life. The secret? Your prep starts now!

Back to the truth. The world is designed to fool you. For example, you look out of your window and watch the sun rising and setting when, in actual fact, the sun pretty much stays where it is, and the earth rotates, giving the illusion of the sun dipping below the horizon.

So if you've been fooled by sunsets and sunrises, just imagine what other tricks your mind is playing on you? But like all magic tricks, once it's been explained, all becomes clear. You might want to think of this book as a cheeky glimpse behind the magician's curtain.

A word of warning before the off – please don't let the pictures and mild humour fool you. This book is backed by a dozen years of hard research and is set in the real world. You can be as positive as you want, but life is like a long stretch of pavement with dog turds littering the way. Our message is watch out for the dog turds of life and avoid them when you can. But there will be times in your life when there's more turd than pavement and you're going to find yourself in a brown and sticky situation.

And, yes, those days will stink to high heaven. This book is for those times too.

So, if the world is already full of it, we promise, no bull from us.

Just One Thing to Remember ...

Admission time. I'm not into Shakespeare or war poems. Yes, just like you, I was force-fed these 'classics' in English and can now reflect on the irony that a subject about reading actually destroyed my love of reading. In the same way that chemistry put me off science and French off languages.

I prefer non-classics, the best of which is Douglas Adams' *The Hitchhiker's Guide to the Galaxy*, a highly recommended comedy sci-fi which reveals the answer to the ultimate question of life, the universe and everything [plot spoiler alert, the answer is 42].

Adams wrote *Hitchhiker* as a 'trilogy in four parts', so we thought we'd borrow his gag. Our four-part trilogy is 'you', 'your impact', 'your future' and 'awesome moments' which, together, build into a mind-blowing manual for the modern-day teenager.

In *Hitchhiker* a person who can stay in control of virtually any situation is somebody who is said to know where his or her towel is, Douglas Adams genius logic being that a towel has immense psychological value. If you pick up an intergalactic hitchhiker who has their towel with them, you will automatically assume that they are also in possession of a toothbrush, flannel, soap, tin of biscuits, flask, compass, map, ball of string, gnat spray, cagoule, space suit, etc. It gives you faith. Anyone who can hitch the length and breadth of the galaxy, rough it, slum it, struggle against terrible odds, win through, and still knows where their towel is, is clearly someone to be reckoned with.

Think of this book as your intergalactic towel. Yes, the modern world is bonkers but that doesn't mean you have to be. This book will give you a certain presence which will make you someone to be reckoned with.

Look around and you'll see a lot of insanity – people who keep doing what they've always done while expecting a different result. Sea squirts. Open your eyes and you'll see burnt out teachers, hassled parents and classmates who continually do the bare minimum. Your ears will pick up a constant low-level grumble. Tune into the feelings and you'll clock a whole herd of people who are a million miles away from feeling as great as they could. It ain't working. If you use the same recipe, you'll get the same cake.

Fast-forward to age 40. What do you want to be? On happy pills, your third marriage and fourth heart murmur?

Or safely in possession of your towel?

Welcome to the Jungle

Menacing advice

'The best thing you can do is get good at being you.'

Dennis the Menace (cartoon hero)

So where do you start with a book that is designed to change your life? Something profound perhaps? A question that gets you to ponder your purpose, your motivation, or the meaning of life?

We'll come to those later. This book is different. And to prove it, we're going to start with a story about Andy's toaster. Like you do.

It's likely that one day you'll get married, or move in with a partner. Andy did. There was a bit of a do, some confetti, a honeymoon and they returned home to a lounge full of unopened prezzies, one of which turned out to be a toaster. This amazing piece of engineering lasted a full 15 years before it eventually gave up and Andy found himself driving to town to buy a new one. He splashed out on a top of the range beast (four slices, brushed silver, cruise control, the works), got home, plugged it in and stood admiringly.

I noticed my 'Toastamatic 2020' came with an instruction booklet. I was intrigued. Somebody had spent time writing this booklet so I owed it to them to have a read. I turned the pages.

Twelve languages! *Impressive*. I decided to just read the English. Found it. The first four pages were health and safety. Don't use the toaster while you're in the bath. Sensible advice, if, I may say, a little over-cautious. Eventually I found the actual instructions on how to make toast. And I'd like to share it with you.

Ready? Here goes ...

- Insert bread (or muffin, bagel, pop-tart, etc.)
- Turn knob to the colour you want it (from snow white to carbon black)
- Push the lever down (unless you're in the bath, remember?)
- Wait
- Toast (muffin, bagel, pop-tart, etc.) pops up
- Remove it, smear it in peanut butter and scoff it

Twelve languages! Someone's put an awful lot of work into that toaster manual. Hang in there; this will make sense in a minute ...

Please rewind to 12 May, 21 years ago. Andy was about to become a dad. His wife was in the maternity ward and he was stroking her forehead. A few complications later and his good lady's being wheeled into theatre for a caesarean. In case you don't know, that means the little un's coming out of the skylight instead of the front door.

Andy gets all dressed up in green surgical gear and follows her in. His wife's on pain relief called an epidural which means she is totally awake but numb from the waist down. Andy resumes forehead stroking duty. He commentates to his wife as the surgeons go about their work. Five minutes and a small incision later, a very small scrap of a child is pulled from her mum's tummy (check out the original *Alien* movie. It was a bit like that).

Thankfully, these are professional people. Cords are cut, the slime wiped off the child and it's handed to Andy. He's a dad. *WooHooo!* Six weeks earlier than expected too! Congratulations from all the team. And then they abandon Andy and his newborn and return to the lady who needs sewing back together.

Andy is left, literally, holding the baby. The as-yet-unnamed child weighs in at a tiny four-and-a-half pounds. It's an emotional moment. Father meets daughter for the very first time. He stares adoringly at his first born. He now knows (but didn't at the time) that human eyeballs don't grow. Babies actually have adult-sized eyeballs. If you stick adult eyes in a four-and-a-half-pound scrap of flesh, they seem massive. So Andy's first words, his momentous welcome to the world? *'It's got owl eyes!'* he exclaims as the tot stares up at him. She's wrapped in a white blanket with a tiny baby foot hanging out. *'And feet...with toes!'* (Andy does appreciate that these first words to his newborn could have been more profound. He will make sure his final words are much better.)

The point of our opening story?

No manual!

19

A toaster, the simplest thing in the world, comes with a comprehensive wad of instructions in a dozen languages, yet Andy's daughter, the most complex piece of kit ever invented, comes with nothing.

Hence, this is our plea. Whoever is bringing you up (mum, dad ... jackals?) – cut them some slack. They are doing their best. We know it might not look that way, and sometimes they'll mess up, but you didn't come with a manual. You're complicated. You have needs and emotions. You have thoughts whizzing around your head and hormones pulsing through your system. You have dreams, secrets, values, fears and feelings.

One day, maybe, you too will become a parent and this paragraph will make perfect sense. Until then, please be kind to those who are doing their best. A hug is nice. If that's too much, try a smile and a kind word to whoever bought you this book.

Tell them you're on page 20 and so far it's the best book ever.

Thank you.

The Story of Your Life

You are a storyteller. Not just you, all humans are. Stories are what link us to our ancestors.

We have stories about everything. *The Gruffalo* is a pretty cool starting place, and then you get into Horrid Henry.

Before you know it, you're treading on heavier territory like Shakespeare or *Heat* magazine.

But you also have a story about you. Your inner story is one of the great classics, although only in your own head. Here's a dirty little secret – you can tell a different and better story. In fact, a change to your inner story is the fastest way to a better you.

Despite what you may have been told, the process of change doesn't have to be psychologically challenging. You can get excited about change if you choose to. Change – it's what you've been doing all your life. Are you the same today as you were yesterday, or last year, or when you were six?

On the same theme, happiness isn't real. Confidence isn't real. The way you feel about yourself isn't real. It's all self-generated, created by the story you tell yourself. This happens silently, inside your head. There's a technical word for it – *thinking!*

Your brain is constructed in such a way as to notice negative stuff (we'll explain more later) hence why you notice bad things and life seems unfair. Problems loom large and, if you're not careful, these problems become your backstory. They become well-rehearsed stories, magnified and re-lived every time you tell them.

But, of course, you're the author. It's your life and your story. You might not be able to change the events that have happened, but you can re-cast yourself as the hero. That changes how you view the past and, spookily, will affect how you approach the future.

Activity: Read all about it!

Imagine you are 40 years old and you've achieved some amazing things. Your local newspaper is writing an article about you.
What would you like the headline to be?

Write the story (what personal battles have you won, what adversity have you learned from, what have you made happen in your life, what are people saying about you, what quote would you give the newspaper reporter, what quote would your teacher give?)

Happy-ology

'Change will not come if we wait for some other person or some other time. We are the ones we've been waiting for. We are the change that we seek.'

Barack Obama (one-time boss of America, very cool)

So our internal story is ours for the changing. We can decide to upgrade ourselves and that decision can happen in an instant. That leads us to a few questions (that only you can answer):

- Well, what is life supposed to be then? Can I re-write my story to be a famous pop star, footballer, scientist or astronaut?

- Why am I here?

- What's the point in having a great imagination?

- What is the secret to life?

- How do I make sure I don't waste it?

- What colour would a Smurf go if you choked it?

- If toast always lands butter-side down, and cats always land on their feet, what happens if you strap toast onto the back of a cat and drop it?

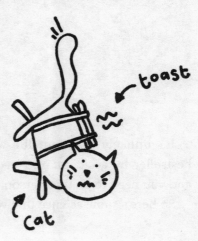

Some of these questions are quite big. Once again, to challenge conventional wisdom, we think you're often asked the wrong question. Next time a relative asks, *'What do you want to be when you grow up?'* smile politely and say, *'That's a great question Aunty Janet, but here's a better one. Try asking me "What kind of person do I want to be when I grow up?" because I'm dead certain of the answer to that one.'*

Activity: Aunty J

So, what's your answer to Aunty J's new improved question?

It's unlikely that your life will unfold as a page-turning bestseller by accident. You need to be an amazing person, and you need to be that person consistently.

So here's some science that will help you along the way.

One of the authors of this book decided to study happy people. That's a pretty cool thing to do and also a very simple idea. In fact, so simple that nobody had ever done it before. Because the 'truth' about psychology is that all the doctors and scientists in the whole world, forever, had done the total opposite.

We've spent billions of hours and squillions of pounds studying unhappy people. Science has always been about finding out why unhappy people are unhappy, depressed people depressed or suicidals suicidal. Then they would invent pills or therapies to make them less unhappy, depressed or suicidal.

That's all well and good but Andy decided to turn the science on its head. He had an idea – what would happen if, for a change, we studied happy folk?

For 12 whole years?

So he did. Andy turned it into an actual job and became a scientist of it. Yes, an actual scientist of happiness. A doctor of joy. He's the exact opposite of a normal doctor.

This simple switch in thinking is a bigger deal than it sounds. It's important because one of the things Andy found out is – get this – happy people aren't rich or famous. They don't have perfect lives. The sun doesn't always shine on them. They live in exactly the same world as everyone else.

Sometimes they get picked last at netball too!

But they have different thinking. That's basically it!

And this book is about that.

Andy calls them '2%ers' – the most positive stand-out people in the population. So when you see the phrase '2%er' that's what we mean – the merry band of folk who have oodles of energy, optimism, happiness and positivity. We're going to reveal who they are, what they're doing that makes them a 2%er and, crucially, what we can learn from them so that we can do what they're doing and live life as a 2%er.

2%ers. Positive folk. The ones who shine. We're gonna tell you how to be one.

Got it?

Good.

Here's the science bit ...

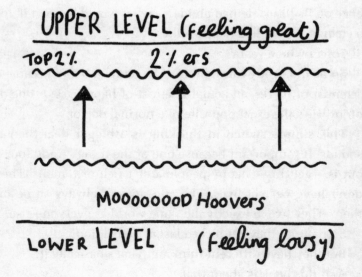

The diagram above explains, as simply as we can, where we're coming from. If, this week, you kept a diary of your emotions and we plotted the result on a graph, you'd have an upper and lower level. So, in a normal week, you will live your life between these two limits of top end 'feel good' and bottom end 'feel lousy'.

You already knew that.

The problem is that far too many people spend far too much of their time in the bottom section. They are not clinically depressed, just stuck in a grumble mode. These are doom and gloom merchants who love to whinge about things. Any topic will do. We call them mood hoovers or dementors. They suck all the energy out of you, leaving you feeling as rubbish as they do.

There's a mass of people in the middle section. They visit the real highs and lows but spend most of their time occupying the safety of the middle ground. If you'll pardon the expression, they swing both ways. Their moods tend to be determined by what happens to them during the day. These are ordinary people who have loads of ordinary days. Most of the time they're 'fine'. We have no axe to grind with these people, but we're certain that they can learn things that will enable them to raise their game. If you've only got 4000 weeks to make a dent in the universe then 'fine' seems a little tame.

And, last but by no means least, there are the top 2%ers. These are people who are significantly more upbeat and positive. To use the pavement analogy, they step into the dog turds, hose themselves down and move forward. The 2%ers are solution focused, energetic and can-do. They tend to get things done (while the mood hoovers roll their eyes and moan that it can't be done) and, crucially, they raise the levels of optimism and energy in those around them. In short, they're good to have around – at school and at home.

These folk are not only significantly happier but they also possess bags more energy. They tend to report feelings of aliveness, vitality and zest.

The problem with 2%ers? The clue's in the name. There aren't enough of them!

Activity: Who's who?

Who are your 2%ers? How do you know?

Who are your mood hoovers? How do you know?

The *'How do you know?'* bit of the activity is crucial. You know your 2%ers are 2%ers because YOU feel great when they're around. Their positivity raises your positivity. And vice versa for the mood hoovers – they suck all the energy out of you leaving you feeling lethargic and drained.

Warning! Please note, we're not talking about bouncing around with jazz hands: *'Woo-Hoo, look at me everybody, I'm a 2%er!'* Charging into school on Monday morning fist pumping into class declaring, *'Don't those weekends drag'*, is not socially acceptable.

We're British. We don't do happy-clappy. We're talking about you being your best self – *consistently* – because why on earth would anyone settle for anything less than being the best they can be?

But tens of millions do.

The 2%er Olympics

The Olympics. Once every four years the best in the world gather somewhere exotic to take on the best in the world.

It's great entertainment but because they're all superb we lose perspective. We know Mr Fast is fast and that he'll beat all the other 'not-quite-so-fasts' by 0.03 of a second. And chucking the javelin 80 metres is a long way. As is hop-skip-jumping 8 metres.

Ditto the Winter Olympics. Shooting headfirst down an icy hill on a baking tray – in less than a minute. It's bonkers and brilliant at the same time.

But we've got an idea to improve what is already the best show on earth ...

We, the TV viewers, need to appreciate just how good these athletes are. So our recommendation is that in every competition, there should be an ordinary guy or girl. Let's call them 'Norman' and 'Norma'.

The Norms have been select-ed because they're totally average. Please take a moment to picture Norman ... slight belly, slumped shoulders, exhausted eyes, hairy back, likes a trip to the pub, works in an office, eats pizza, has bad dan-druff. And Norma? Same but an even hairier back.

NORMAN   NORMA

The Norms have got their work cut out because they're going to have to compete in every single event. So, as Mr Fast and all those other not-so-fasts stretch their chests at the finish line, Norm is rising from the blocks. As Mrs Swim stretches her exhausted fingers towards the end of the 100m butterfly, Norma is adjusting her goggles and stepping down the ladder. As Mr Dive completes a triple somersault and lands without a splash, Norm bombs it from 25 metres, soaking the spectators. As Mrs Javelin nails a 65-metre throw, Norma mistimes hers, accidentally spearing one of the judges. *Oops!*

But there are serious points to our new Olympic rules. First, it's easy to be one of the Norms. It takes no training or dedication to achieve averageness. And second, it's not about the Olympics or, indeed, Norman. It's about life, and you. If there was an Olympics for attitude, positivity, optimism, enthusiasm, passion and happiness – would you be normal?

If so, we'd like you to raise your sights to gold medal standard.

Welcome to the world of the 2%ers where rising above average means you'll stand out for all the right reasons.

Hopefully you are now getting what a 2%er actually is? It's a new improved you!

In fact, here's some good news. *You already are one!*
Sometimes!

Think back to the last time you had a brilliant day? A day when you felt like you could take on the world. Think about all the good feelings you had. Invincibility, happiness, joy, positivity, energy, passion ... you were being a 2%er.

Activity: You on a good day...

Describe yourself on that day (i.e., tell a story of you at your best). What happened, how did you feel, how did those around you feel?

The truth is that we all visit these fantastic times on a random basis. But what if we could learn to feel like that more often? What if your good days were less dependent on what was happening *to* you and more dependent on what thoughts were happening *within* you?

What if we could learn some simple principles so that feeling great became a habit?

More good news. You can, and it's dead simple.

Back to the 2%ers diagram, the difference between you at the bottom and top of the emotional spectrum is a game-changer. Our promise is that you will have a happier, more rewarding life if you live it as a top 2%er. Your relationships will be easier, life will be more fun, you'll smile more and the chances are, you'll live longer!

Let's prove it ...

Activity: You who?

We're going to stick you in Dr Who's TARDIS and send you 20 years into the future. We want you to write two accounts of your life:

Firstly, imagine that you've spent 20 years being a mood hoover. School was tough, homework was a pain (so you hardly did any), revision was boring (so you couldn't be bothered), you messed around at school and did the bare minimum. Stepping out into your future, please write an account of how life has turned out. For example, if you've had a negative attitude and bare-minimum work ethic for 20 years, what kind of job are you doing? What's your lifestyle? Where do you live? Who are you with? What kind of house, car, phone, etc? What do people say about you?

My life, age xx, as a mood hoover ...

Second, we want you to write another future, this time having stepped out of the TARDIS as a 2%er. That's 20 years of positivity, growth and a go-getting attitude. Imagine, the best version of you for 20 years? So, same questions as above, write about your future:

My life, age xx, as a 2%er ...

This book is peppered with dirty little truths, and here's a hard hitting one. Not everyone fulfils their potential. In fact, most people waste it.

Either of those futures can be yours. The question at this stage is, *How badly do you want the bright one?*

Botheredness

We've all seen bags of peanuts with a warning *'Might contain nuts'*. And in a toy shop I saw a child's Superman cape that came with a warning: *'Wearing of this garment doesn't allow you to fly'.*

And, in a similar vein, we reckon it's OK to have a positive mindset, but let's not go too far. Let's not be ridiculous about positivity. There are many instances where it's perfectly okay to be downbeat, cautious and pessimistic. If I get run over by a bus and sustain a head injury I don't want the bus driver to be all smiley and positive: *'Roll him over. I can see he's bleeding on the brain. Anyone got a penknife, I need to open him up and perform brain surgery. I've seen them do it on Casualty.'*

No thanks. That's the dangerous cloud-cuckoo end of the positivity spectrum. We're positioned a notch or two down from there at the 'optimistic but realistic' end. The part of the spectrum that allows you to stand out a mile for the right reasons. The exact point on the 'awes-ometer' of being your best self, *consistently and appropriately.*

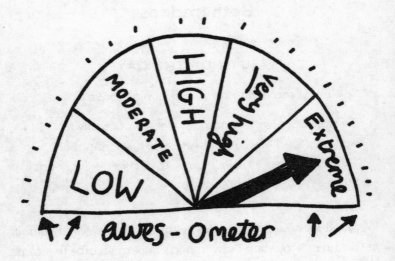

METAPHOR OF THE DAY: DIRTY WINDOWS

A young couple moved into a swanky apartment in a new neighbourhood. They sat in their kitchen having breakfast, watching the world go by. The woman saw her neighbour pegging out the washing. *'That laundry's not very clean,'* she tutted. *'She either needs a new washing machine or better washing powder.'*

Other than crunching on his toast, her husband remained silent.

His wife's comment was exactly the same the next day. And the next. *'Why on earth is that woman hanging out dirty washing?'* she sighed in disgust.

'She needs lessons in basic hygiene!'

And her husband crunched, knowingly.

On the fourth day his wife plonked herself at the breakfast table with a gleeful smile. 'At last,' she said, pointing at their neighbour's washing line. Her husband followed her gaze to the neatly arranged clothes line where the whites sparkled and the colours shone. 'All of a sudden she seems to have learned to clean properly.'

And her husband broke his silence. 'I got up early this morning and cleaned our windows.'

And so it is with life. We view the world from inside our head. It's easy to be critical of other people, but this book isn't about them.

It's easy for our windows to become grimy. So, to stretch the vision metaphor just a little bit too far, we don't want you to go all 'rose tinted'. Not everything in the world is good and bright and fantastic. But, if you follow our advice and view the world through our 'positive tinted' spectacles, the world's a lot brighter than you think.

For too many people, their natural habitat lies in the middle of the diagram and they visit the 2% heights occasionally (we call those occasions 'Saturdays'). We've met adults who've been in the bottom third of the diagram for decades! This doesn't make them sad or horrible people, just a bit stuck. Being negative has become a habit... they don't even know they're doing it.

Let's not pull any punches. The biggest reason why most people are a million miles away from feeling brilliant, is that it's *easier* to be negative. It takes no effort whatsoever to conform to 'normal', and if 'normal' means we gripe about school, teachers and the news and we take to social media to make nasty/sharp comments then so be it. We like to fit in. Everybody else is doing it, right? It's so easy to be negative and join in with all the bad stuff in the world.

Our argument is simple: it doesn't matter what anyone else is doing. *It matters what you are doing.*

Please compose yourself before reading the next sentence. *Upgrading to a 2%er is not easy.* Your brain actually works in the opposite direction. It's a problem spotting machine. It's considerably more challenging to be upbeat, happy and positive. And because it's hard work and it takes practice, most people can't be bothered.

Our message is *get bothered*. There's nothing more important that you'll ever do than spread positive, upbeat, energetic, passionate vibes. You'll feel better for it. And, crucially, those around you will respond in a positive manner. We're promising that if you learn to be a 2%er and then do it for the next 80 years it will change your life. No kid gloves here. We're not messing. We're not talking about it having a marginal effect around the edges of your existence, we're telling you that being a 2%er (and staying there) will fundamentally alter your future. You will get markedly different results in terms of exams, relationships, uni, apprenticeship, career, life, happiness ... just about everything you do will yield better results when you do it as a positive human being.

But there's an even better challenge ahead. A challenge so exciting that it makes my skin tingle (or is that just my dermatitis again?). The real question is, over the next 80 years, *how many people can you take with you?* How many people can you influence in a positive way? How many can you inspire?

Boy, that sounds like worthwhile work.

EXTRA UMPH

'The difference between "try" and "triumph" is just a little "umph".'

Activity: Regrets, I have a few ...

What, for you, is 'success'?

Interviews with the elderly do not report that people regret the things they have done, but rather, people talk about the things they regret *not* having done. What are your thoughts on this?

What are the most important things life has taught you (so far)?

List 20 things you want to do before you die.

That list of 20. It's a really big deal

Here's something Andy used in another book but it's so powerful it bears repeating. Oh, and you might need to sit down for it ...

A doctor decided to ask her patients what they enjoyed in life, and what gave it meaning. All well and good, except this doctor happened to work with terminally ill children. 'Terminal' is just the worst word. In an airport a terminal is where your journey ends. In a hospital, that journey is life. These children ain't going to get better. Ever. They're not going to get to enjoy the pleasure of being an adult.

Here are some of the children's responses.

First: none said they wished they'd watched more TV, zero said they wished they'd spent more time on Facebook, zilch said they enjoyed fighting with others and not one of them enjoyed hospital.

Interestingly, lots mentioned their pets and almost all mentioned their parents, often expressing worry or concern such as, *'I hope mum will be ok. She seems sad'* and *'Dad mustn't worry. He'll see me again one day in heaven maybe.'*

All of them loved ice-cream. *Fact!* Also, they all loved books or being told stories, especially by their parents.

Many wished they had spent less time worrying about what others thought of them, and valued people who just treated them 'normally'. For example, *'My real friends didn't care when my hair fell out.'*

Many of them loved swimming, and the beach. Almost all of them valued kindness above most other virtues: *'Jonno gave me half his sandwich when I didn't eat mine. That was nice,'* and *'I like it when that kind nurse is here. She's gentle. And it hurts less.'*

All of them loved people who made them laugh: *'The boy in the next bed farted! Hahaha!'* [laughter relieves pain]

And finally, they ALL valued time with their family. Nothing was more important. *'Mum and dad are the best!'* *'My sister always hugs me tight'* *'No one loves me like mummy loves me!'*

Look here dear reader, these are very big messages indeed. If you can't be bothered to listen to anything else in this book, then please listen to children who are arriving at the final destination of their very short lives.

If we're allowed to summarize, it'd be something like this: Be kind. Read

Eat ME!

more books. Spend time with your family. Crack jokes. Fart in bed. Go to the beach. Hug your dog.

Oh ... and eat ice-cream. Often.

Living Your Dream (Or Your Nightmare?)

THINKING BIG

'There is no passion to be found playing small – in settling for a life that is less than the one you are capable of living.'

Nelson Mandela (unfairly banged up for 30 years and then, on release, had no regrets. A proper 2%er)

Let's go back to those who inhabit the rarefied atmosphere of the upper 2%. They're only human so they experience downtime, but their natural habitat is close to the upper reaches of how fab they can feel. They have energy, positivity, radiance and often wear a smile. They're great to have around because they light up the room. Who the heck are these weirdoes ... I mean 'positive people'? What do they do that makes them so happy? And what can we learn from them that we can actually put into practice in our own lives?

GOOD QUESTION

'Why be "ordinary", when you can choose to be "extra-ordinary"? Why live life in black and white when it can be colour?'

Richard Wilkins (Minister of Inspiration)

Please don't fall into the trap of thinking this is all about positive thinking. I once heard a school assembly where the guest speaker was whipping the teenagers into a frenzy of getting them to believe that they could do anything so long as they did some positive thinking. Sorry matey, but no. The 5 foot 2 lad in year 11 is never going to be a basketball star, the large girl in year 9 isn't going to be a jockey, and the nervous year 7 girl (the one with shaking hands) ain't going to be a brain surgeon.

It's safe to say that positive thinking won't let you do 'anything'. However, it will enable you to do 'everything' better than negative thinking will. When you walk into a dark room and flick the light switch, the room is instantly lit. Flipping the switch did not generate the electricity; it released the electricity that was already there.[1] Positive thinking is a bit like the light switch – it releases the amazing abilities you already have.

---

1 In the interests of making your head hurt, what if lightbulbs work in the opposite way to how we think? Instead of lighting the room, they're sucking in the dark?

Once again, the truth sounds harsh. Not everybody gets to be an astronaut when they grow up. Very few get to be footballers or gamers or YouTubers either. There are a lot of people who are stuck in dead-end jobs, just about making ends meet, living a life of nightmares rather than dreams.

Brilliant lives don't just happen. Being a 2%er doesn't just happen. We've spent 12 years studying these amazing people and, guess what, being a 2%er is a *learned behaviour*. They have strategies in place that enable them to flourish.

Activity: Picture this

What three words or phrases describe who you would like to be as a person?

When you're living the words above, what do you:
Look like?

Sound like?

Feel like?

How often are you at your absolute best? (Honestly.)

What's stopping you?

Controlling the Controllables

This book is like learning to swim. First you dip your toes in to test the temperature, then you lower yourself down the ladder to splash around in the shallow end before you gradually gravitate to jumping into the deep end.

So here's the toe in the water bit. The 90:10 principle is a general theme around which life is based. Like with everything else in this book, we've boiled it down to its bare bones.

10% of life is made up of what happens to you.

90% of life is decided by *how you react* to the 10%.

What does this mean?

Budgie smugglers on? We're going in.

We really have no control over 10% of what happens to us. Yet again, we're back to the dog turds on the pavement of life. At various points in your life, things will go wrong, sometimes dreadfully so. A class test will go badly, you'll fail an exam, you'll flunk your driving test, the love of your life will turn you down, you'll get stupid amounts of homework, your mum will nag you, you'll get an epic zit on your forehead ... you have no control over this 10%.

The other 90% is different. *You* determine the other 90%. This is where the choice to be a 2%er kicks in. The key factor is *your reaction* to events that happen around you.

You cannot control the ridiculous homework deadline, but you can control how you *think* about it. You cannot control the queue at the supermarket, but you can control how you stand there. The zit isn't great news but you can laugh about it instead of letting it ruin your life.

Think about the following step-by-step example:

You wake up and go through your morning routine. You scroll through your social media as you tuck into your Rice Krispies and notice someone has said horrible things about you. *What? Why? How?* You're devastated. You immediately go off on one, sending an angry reply and feeling full of hate.

Your head is spinning as you grab your bag and storm out of the house. Glued to your mobile, you check the collection of comments as you walk to school. You manage to post a couple of hates back at the person who started it.

You have a bad attitude in registration and can't concentrate in lesson 1. Your teacher gets angry because you're on the phone and you're just plain rude, huffing and puffing as you reluctantly put the phone back in your bag. You've forgotten your PE kit and Food Tech ingredients so, quite frankly, you're having a bit of a mare. Lunchtime is spent alone, seething, posting negatives about the person who started it. Post-lunch, your phone is finally confiscated and you have to collect it from the head's office after school.

A bad day all round. You get home in a foul mood, poisoning your family with your scowl. You're already dreading tomorrow.

The key question is, '*Why did you have a bad day?*'

A) Did the negative comment cause it?

B) Did one of your teachers cause it?

C) Or getting your phone confiscated?

D) Or did you cause it?

If we follow the 90:10 principle, the answer is D. You had no control over what happened with the comment. However, how you reacted in those five seconds is what caused your bad day.

Consider the same scenario but with a different reaction:

You wake up and go through your morning routine. You scroll through your social media as you tuck into your Rice Krispies and notice someone has said horrible things about you.

You stop to consider for a moment. It's uncalled for, unfair even. But, hey, they're probably having a bad day. You realize that a lot of the negative stuff on 'anti-social media' says more about those who spit the bile than it does about you.

Chill. They might be having a bad day but you're sure not going to. You finish your Rice Krispies and check your bag instead. Ingredients and PE kit ... so off you go, head held high. You meet a couple of your mates at the school gates and laugh things off. To be fair, most people haven't even noticed so you've soon forgotten it and have thrown yourself into baking cupcakes.

At the school gates, you walk past the neg head and in a delicious twist of fate, give them a smile and offer a cake. No words are necessary. They take it and you win, by a zillion miles, your dignity and day intact.

You get home, in a great mood, and your family has a fabulous evening. Tomorrow is going to be good too.

Notice the difference? The same start to the day, but two different outcomes. The key point is to make the link between the 'trigger' (in this case, a nasty comment) and your 'reaction' (anger in scenario 1 and calm in scenario 2).

David Taylor calls it the gap of infinite possibilities. The 90:10 principle is very simple yet very few people actually apply it to their lives. We cannot control the event, but we're absolutely in charge of how we choose to react. And the top 2%ers react differently. Therefore, they tend to get more positive results and better lives!

The gap of infinite possibilities is so powerful, we'd like you to work through a few examples, just to prove the point.

Activity: Mind the gap

In the following situations, write down how the negative and positive version of you would react:

You're a little bit off task in a lesson and your teacher asks you to stop chatting to your friend and crack on with your work.

The mood hoover me would:	The 2% me would:

You're in a boring lesson

The mood hoover me would:	The 2% me would:

You disagree with someone

The mood hoover me would:	The 2% me would:

You do badly in a test

The mood hoover me would:	The 2% me would:

Your mum's asked you to nip to the shop and there's a 20-minute queue at the checkout

The mood hoover me would:	The 2% me would:

You're on holiday and it's raining	
The mood hoover me would:	The 2% me would:

You've been dragged along to meet an elderly relative	
The mood hoover me would:	The 2% me would:

Alohomora

Here are our brand-spankingly new 'Five Levels of Teen-ageism'™ (that we've just this minute Trade Marked, just in case). Please note, the levels are nothing to do with your academic ability.

Nothing. Zilch.

If you drew it, it'd look a bit like a wobbly Jenga, something like this ...

53

5 LEVELS of *Teenageism:* ™

5. **WOW** zone

4. *botheredness* zone

3. BOG STANDARD zone

2. meh zone

1. OANGER zone

↑ brand-Spankingly NEW

Have a read and pigeon-hole yourself:

Level 1, the danger zone, is dire. Properly dangerous. It's reserved for young people who come to school because the law says they have to. Level 1s are the minimalists, dragging themselves between lessons and being disengaged when they finally arrive. They're the ones who always raise their hands with *'Miss, can I go to the toilet'* because spending time loitering in the loo is the most exciting part of their day. [Note, their teachers are happy to let them go.] Disruptive to their classmates, level 1s make teachers wonder why they ever bothered training to be a teacher. Their only after-school club is detention. Danger Zone teenagers often come from Danger Zone families and educational psychologists will find all sorts of excuses for why they are what they are.

Let's cut the excuses. You can trot out 'bad parenting' or 'terrible thing has happened' but, deep down, there are no excuses for rudeness, lateness and couldn't-care-lessedness. If your parents are rubbish, you still have choices. You can choose to live the stereotype or rise above it. Level 1s are a terrible waste of human potential. Unless they change, they're going nowhere. These are the ones you need to unfollow in real life.

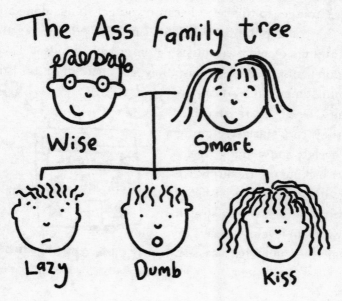

The Ass family tree

Wise

Smart

Lazy

Dumb

Kiss

Level 2s are more upbeat. They have a pulse, but not on Mondays or Tuesdays. These teenagers perk up from Wednesday afternoon because *'It's all downhill from here'*. They come alive in spurts, mostly in the lessons that they like (and for the teachers they like). So, in some lessons they shift from *having* to work to *wanting* to work. However, don't be fooled, as soon as the going gets tough there's plenty of tutting, rolling of eyes and outbursts of *'It's not fair'*. Can be quite vocal in lessons in a *'Miss, I don't get it'*, kind of way. They have a form of 'moaning Tourettes'. It's a habit. It's easy to be a level 2. The earlier they break into levels 3 and 4, the better their life chances.

Level 3 is where young people can really start gaining traction. Currently residing in bog-standard, but there's hope. You get to this level because you get things done and you have a reputation for delivering. *Sometimes!* It's the beginnings of what scientists call a growth mindset. Level 3s don't mind school because they 'get' that education isn't a punishment, it's an oppor-

tunity. Level 3s are saveable. If they can start stretching to levels 4 and 5, things really start picking up. Health warning: it's a whole lot easier to join the level 2s than stretch upwards to level 4. Always do what's best, not what's easiest.

it's an opportunity!

Teens at level 4 tend to get along with almost all the teachers (there might be one whose lessons are drab, but the level 4s will tolerate these lessons, knowing that they won't have to study them at apprenticeship, A-level or degree). Level 4s are great to have in class because they crack on with the right amount of banter and effort. They've developed a healthy amount of 'botheredness'. School is to be enjoyed and, as such, level 4s have a good-sized friendship group and half a dozen proper besties. Helpful, polite and positive, the level 4s are milking school for the right reasons – personal growth and development. Teachers say nice things about them in the staffroom. Level 4s have twigged that laziness pays off now but effort pays off in the future – hence their futures are bright.

Level 5s have nailed it. Plenty of effort, but with a healthy dollop of social skills so they're kind of cool with it? A wide friendship group, and enough besties to make school a lovely place to be. Level 5s realize that education is paid for via the tax system so although it doesn't cost anything to go to school, it actually costs the government £5,000 per pupil per year to fund their education. Level 5 thinking is *'If some-one's investing £5k a year in me for 13 years, that's a cool 65 grand's worth of education, so I'd better make the most of it'*. And they do. Level 5s listen and behave. They've developed growth mindset thinking which means that they've twigged that hard work pays off in the long run. They support their teachers, even thanking them when they've delivered a brilliant lesson. They're not nerdy or geeky – the learning is still a challenge – but they rise to it. Level 5s are the antidote to level 1s. They are the reason why teachers hang in there – because they're lovely. Guaranteed a rosy future.

Remember, the level you reach has nothing to do with how 'clever' you are. Each level represents a huge increase in commitment over the one before. Stepping up from one level to the next is all about choice and effort. The gulf between level 1 (coming to school because you have to) and level 5 (coming to school because you want to) has almost incalculable benefits in terms of the effort you will give. Of course, our five levels are a short-hand description. Young people might be at different levels on different days, or in different lessons, or for different teachers. The difference is that level 5ers have achieved a consistency of effort and atti-tude across *all* lessons and with *all* teachers.

Here's the frustration. Your school will be putting in loads of extra support for the level 1s and 2s. So while your level 4s and 5s get the standard £5,000 a year (that pays for teach-ers, classrooms, computers, heating, lighting, loo roll, etc), the kids who misbehave will be getting double or triple spent on them. Your school will have a special room where the baddies go. In this room, they get 1:1 support which is ridiculously expensive.

It brings us back to the truths revealed in this chapter; it doesn't matter what anyone else is doing, it matters what you're doing. Do it better than you have to – inhabit the 2% version of yourself. And, of course, the 90:10 principle means you cannot control circumstances, but you can learn how to respond positively to whatever life throws at you. These responses accumulate into a great big thing called 'habits' – things that you repeatedly do.

That brings us full circle. Climbing the wobbly Jenga mountain is not about 'magic' or 'wishing'. Your life becomes the story of what you repeatedly do.

End of Part 1 challenge: 'Inspiry Diary'

One of the quickest ways to feel amazing is to do a good deed for someone else. You don't need a wand or an 'Alohomora', random acts of kindness will work their magic and open up a world of possibilities.

So here is the challenge: over the next week carry out at least one random act of kindness a day and make a note of it and how you felt. Here are a few examples to get your brain going ...

- Hold a door open for someone
- Help a teacher with their bags
- Praise someone for who they are or what they did
- Say a genuine 'thank you' to your teacher for all the effort they put into helping you achieve, despite the fact you don't deserve it at times
- Say a heartfelt 'thanks' to whomever makes your tea
- Say three nice things on social media

So, do them and then fill out what you did on the next page (your 'Inspiry Diary') and how you felt afterwards. Then take a photo of it and tweet or email it to us so we can get a massive collection of how great teenagers really are...

Your 'Inspiry Diary'

Day 1

Day 2

Day 3

Day 4

Day 5

I feel ...

BRILLIANT IMPACT

BRILLIANT IMPACT

Brace yourself for Part 2 which is full of monkeys and bears. It also has a liberal sprinkling of the F-word (no, not that one!) and we introduce the notion that a thought isn't a thing.

We challenge you to get your backside off the self-imposed naughty step of life and introduce you to the number 1 thing that you can do to get everyone on your side. Clue, it's absolutely NOT what you're expecting.

After we've consoled you with 'it's okay to not be okay' we kind of pull the rug from under your feet with the sad story of Bea. Yes dear reader, it's easy to slip into a routine that doesn't serve you well.

Speaking of which, your routines are created by your brain, so we tell you a little bit about how it works. Don't worry, there are no big words. Plot spoiler, the teenage brain isn't fully developed. You're like a half-baked cake.

This section also contains a warning: running naked on the beach age 2 is fine. It's not recommended if you're 14. Just sayin'.

Then we dish out some top advice that will help you roll with the punches. There's a cool bit about how to win the lottery (*100% guaranteed!*) and how to make your parents and teachers go 'wow!'

We finish by explaining why Swedish people are so happy (it's actually nothing to do with naked saunas) and send you on an all expenses paid holiday of a lifetime.

Seatbelt time again. This time you might need to adopt the brace position ...

I'M POSSIBLE

'The only way of discovering the limits of the possible is to venture a little way past them into the impossible.'

Arthur C. Clarke (British writer, inventor, under-sea explorer and futurist)

Superhero You

There are plenty of superheroes on the TV. Far fewer in real life.

Wouldn't it be awesome if you were one of the select few? One of the secret superheroes, blending in to normal life but with a whole host of powers that you could unleash.

Add your name in the [spaces] below to get a feel for super-hero status:

1. Is it a bird? Is it a plane? No, it's [*insert your name here*]

2. When the Bogeyman goes to sleep he checks under his bed for [   ]

3. [   ] counted to infinity. Twice.

4. [   ] gave Mona Lisa that smile.

5. ['s] calendar goes straight from 31 March to 2 April. No-one fools [   ]

6. Superman owns a pair of [   ] pyjamas.

7. [   ] sleeps with a night light. Not because [   ] is afraid of the dark but because the dark is afraid of [   ].

8. Once a cobra bit [   ]. After three days of excruciating pain, the cobra died.

Monkey Business

What's the single biggest thing you can do to get other people to warm to you – the silver bullet of human popularity and connection?

Like in all the best TV series, we'll leave that one dangling for the next episode. All will be revealed. Be sure to keep reading!

In the meantime, you know that inner voice? The negative chatter in your head? The self-critical, self-sabotaging one? The *'I can't do it'*, *'I'm not clever enough'*, *'What will people think of me?'*, *'I'll never be as good as so-and-so'* voice.

Also known as the *'If you spoke to anyone else like you speak to yourself, you wouldn't have any friends'* voice.

Just in case you were wondering, everyone has that voice. We're going to help you get to grips with it in Part 4 but, for now, we want to gently make you aware of it. Particularly to notice it and realize the voice isn't real. Yes, we know it sounds real and it seems real. But it's a thought, and thoughts aren't 'things'.

You have a public self, the outer-facing version of you. Think of this as you centre stage, with the lights on. Everyone can see and hear the public you. It can be a bit of an act. And then there's the private self, the lights-off version of you. Nobody else can see or hear this version. This is you, backstage. The version of you that knows how you truly feel. This private self is often self-critical and lacking in confidence. Prof Steve Peters calls it your inner chimp. Chill. Almost everyone has a private self that is their own worst critic.

The problem arises when your private self, the critical 'Oh my gosh, I'm such a douche' version of you, starts to show in your behaviours.

I've watched a few parenting TV programmes in which the parents have introduced a naughty step – a place where their kids can sit and reflect on their bad behaviour. All too often, the private version of you (i.e. the you in your head) is permanently on the naughty step. Because of the way the brain operates, most people are punishing themselves.

Please believe us when we tell you, you are not an idiot, you are not stupid and the world is not against you. In fact, you are amazing! Sure, you've made a few mistakes and said some stupid things. Here's the shock horror unbelievable truth ... *everyone messes up.*

Just because you've messed up doesn't mean you *are* messed up.

Remember, you are the best version of you on the planet. So get off your self-imposed naughty step. Everyone else has forgotten, or didn't care in the first place. They're too busy sitting on their own naughty step. If, in your head, you have to sit somewhere, sit where the 2%ers sit, on the positive step.

In Part 1, we learned that your thoughts and feelings are driven by your inner story. Everyone has a fear of making mistakes (because mistakes frighten you) so you've become fearful of fear. This is when you have to be bold. Please believe us when we tell you that most people who are living within their comfort zone are incredibly uncomfortable.

GOOD ADVICE

Get comfortable with feeling uncomfortable.

So, if you fancy experimenting with an upgraded version of yourself, it might be useful to think of your negative inner voice going on holiday for a couple of weeks. Send your inner chimp away to the zoo, leaving you free to be the brilliant version of yourself. What a fabulous opportunity! While the slightly rubbish version of you is swinging on the tyres or throwing poo at the public, the 2%er version will be shining at school and home. Enjoy inhabiting the brilliant version of you 24/7. Smile more, laugh a lot, shine in class, try your very best, thank your teachers, be kind, help out at home, do your homework without grumbling (and do it superbly so your teacher goes 'wow!'), say nice things about people behind their back, walk tall, be confident, raise your hand in class, have a go, role model positivity ...

happy holidays

If it doesn't work out, you can always revert back to the rubbish version of you. But we're pretty sure that after two weeks of being a 2%er you'll want to keep your negative inner chimp where it belongs, safely behind bars.

THE TRUEST THING EVER

'You cannot be anything you want to be – but you can be a LOT more of who you already are.'

Tom Rath (Author. Tom also happens to have a rare genetic disorder that causes cancer cells to appear in various parts of his body. This, I would imagine, is far from ideal.)

Learning to be your own bestie is a battle worth fighting. You'll still mess up, but instead of sitting on the naughty step, you can think a better thought. So instead of *'What an idiot for messing up in Biology'* you say *'I messed up in Biology, so what have I just learned?'* Or simply, *'What will I do differently next time?'*

Experiment with your chimp. See if you can notice it, and tame it. Maybe you'll start noticing when other people have been taken over by their chimps? Either way, your inner voice is such a big deal that we're going to come back to it later.

Activity: Your telegram from the King

It's your 100th birthday and there's a big family party in your honour. Someone is going to stand up and say a few words about you. What would you like them to say?

The F-Word

This book has adult themes, so brace yourself for some liberal use of the f-word. In fact, we use the f-word all the time and have grown to love it: **failure**.

Not failure the result: flunking the test, being dumped by text, failing the interview, losing the game.

But failure the *process*: learning, improving, becoming fighting-fit, installing effectiveness, building experience, getting really really good, broadening, apologizing, widening, gaining wisdom, picking yourself up and smiling as you try again.

Rising stronger.

Yeah, that bit.

The whole process of being awesome requires lots and lots of crappy failure. And, of course, you don't like it: you want approval, love, success, victory, results, accolades. *But hang on a minute: no, you don't.* If you really want to grow, discover who the heck you are and where your limits are, you'll be needing to push your boundaries.

Seriously, if you want to start creating your greatest work and achieving personal bests, you'll need to be prepared to fail. Repeatedly. With tears at times. But stay in the game. The right result will be getting closer.

Change is renewal. Staying the same means stagnation.

UNARGUABLY CORRECT

'Character cannot be developed in ease and quiet. Only through experience of trial and suffering can the soul be strengthened, ambition inspired, and success achieved.'

Helen Keller (Google her. She just knew, okay?)

In a book that's essentially about positive emotions, we think it's important to acknowledge that being sad is an important part of being happy. A life of unbridled joy would be bizarre. A permanent high? You'd lose perspective. Lows are inevitable. Welcome them. Let an occasional bad day into your life, show it around, then show it the door.

We're not from the Rah-Rah-Woo-Hoo school of positivity. *'Yippee, grandma's died! What a great opportunity to have some sandwiches and cake at a funeral,'* will get you noticed for all the wrong reasons.

In the example above, a better reaction to your grandma's demise might be a heart full of sadness that lingers for a while but is replaced by pride at having had such a wonderful person in your life.

The result: you will experience grief, but be better able to move on in good time.

It's perfectly OK to have a bad time. Sometimes there's no alternative but to sit down and have a huge sob. Crying serves a purpose. It lets stuff out. It shows the world you're hurt and it's the start of the repairing process. It can be a bit messy but it's your safety valve.

If you fall down and cut your knee, it bleeds for a bit, scabs over, starts itching and eventually you spend an entire evening picking your scab off and, hey presto, brand new pink skin, good as new.

Your physical system repairs itself, and the same applies to your emotional self.

All human beings come with a standard issue of 'ordinary magic', an in-built ability to heal your heart and mind.

The mind–body system will repair itself naturally, with time, if you let it. In fact, controversial as it may sound, you will heal quicker and better if you allow yourself to feel pain and sadness. The older generation have invented the term 'snowflake generation', which is a condescending way of suggesting that you guys are brittle. The argument is that you're okay when things are going well but when the going gets tough, young people fall apart. 'Generation snowflake' is a reference to the fact that young people are seen as a bit melty.

When bad stuff happens (which it will), it's easy to take the emotional pain away with medication. Even worse, the suggestion is that you might talk yourself into depression, anxiety, panic or school phobia. Your brain can be hijacked by strong emotions. The result is that you can take medication, or simply remove yourself from school. The problem is that these remedies are simply masking the situation. By never dealing head-on with the problem you are never learning to deal with the problem, so when it comes round again (which it will), you will be back to square one.

If you'll allow us to tell it like it is? You have a problem? Congratulations. *Only dead people don't have problems!* Happiness is not the absence of problems. Any problem is a chance to change for the better (it might be heavily disguised, but it's a gift all the same).

TRUE (AND VERY SAD) STORY

A charity fought for the release of a circus bear. Beatriz was an eight-year old brown bear who had been trained to dance for the Russian public. She was well-travelled, secured in her 12-foot cage.

After securing her release the charity team took her to the forest and opened her cage door.

Beatriz was enticed out into the vast wilderness of the Russian mountains and spent the rest of her life pacing 12 feet by 12 feet.

Running scared of failure means you never really go for it. You live a safe but mediocre life. The boundaries you erect to protect you from the world also act as barriers that stop you fully experiencing the world. Like Beatriz, you spend 4000 weeks pacing up and down in a self-imposed mental prison cell.

The bars to your mental prison cell are not real. You've created them. We dare you to set yourself free!

Ripples

Previously, in 'Awesome Teenager' ... (you need to re-read that in a deep Netflix boxset voice), we asked you for the #1 thing that shoots you to the top of the popularity stakes.

It's probably not what you imagine? It's not confidence, nor intelligence, good looks nor charm. It's simply that you like most people. Yes, that's it! If everyone in your class writes down a list of people they like, the key to your like-ability is that the list of 'who you like', is longer. Of course, your list has to be genuine. You actually have to like people and, if you do, you become genuinely interested in them and in a bizarre twist of the universe, they will also like you.

This points to something that most people are unaware of, spending their entire lives blinkered to the wonders of human potential – your attitude to another will help to shape that person's world. By our attitude to the other person we help to determine the scope and colour of their world; we make it large or small, bright or drab, rich or dull, threatening or secure. What's more, we help to shape their world not by complicated theories, but by our own attitude towards that person.

Your emotions are very leaky. When you're feeling amazing, your amazingness passes on to 3 degrees of people removed from you. It's actually quite simple, but let me ram the point home. Feeling happy is good for you. You already know that. On a happy day, you feel alive, energized and able to take on the world. But your feelings are bigger than you. Anyone you meet will catch your happiness by a minimum of 16%. Plain simple English? Your family, friends and teachers will all catch your happiness – but it doesn't stop there. Your teacher is 16% happier (because you've been a joy to have in class and she's caught your happiness) and she goes home to her family. Her family is now 10% happier (you haven't met your teacher's family, but it's your happiness they're feeling).

But your happiness virus doesn't stop there either! Let's assume your teacher's teenage son then pops out to the supermarket to buy some milk. He's 10% happier, so has a bit of banter with the lady on the checkout, and she's now 6% happier. And, no, you've not been anywhere near the supermarket.

So your happiness contagion has spread to your teacher by 16%, to her family by 10% and to the checkout operator by 6%. And, of course, you're creating this happiness ripple with everyone you meet.

This is why we're so excited! If you truly get what we're on about, and can be bothered to practise being a 2%er until it sticks, you are a walking tsunami of positivity. To be frank, we're struggling to think of anything more important that you'll ever do and we're tempted to stop the book right here.

And we would have stopped right there if it wasn't for one nasty little problem. In the same way that the theory of playing the piano is relatively straightforward, but actually playing the piano can seem devilishly complicated, being a 2%er is great in theory, but life isn't a theory. It's a very practical thing, and devilishly complicated to boot.

Exactly like the piano example, being a 2%er gets easier with practice. If you start now, you'll be a grand master of awesomeness in a couple of years.

Your Brain is Back to Front

The human being is built with lots of design faults, not least of which is the fact that boys have nipples. I mean, what's the point? And then, just as you reach the age when you start fancying people, your skin explodes into a zit-fest, destroying your chances.

Thank God, or evolution, or whatever.

Human beings are social creatures. Yes, we acknowledge that teenage-hood is associated with spending a bunch of time alone, in your room, but you are a social animal, we promise. Have you noticed that, at school, you feel an overwhelming need to fit in? Adolescence is when the moorings of young people begin to shift. It's always been that way. In fact, it's supposed to be that way. Our hunch is that the age of this shift is coming earlier, often before young people are ready for it.

Your brain develops from the back to the front. So basically, all the motor skills such as balance, walking, riding a bike, writing and bowel control come early (we recognize that most teenage boys still struggle with the latter) but the front parts of your brain are not quite sorted until your mid-20s. You're a work in progress! So what do these undeveloped frontal brain parts do? Rationalizing, organizing, planning and thinking ahead, that's what.

That's why you're so disorganized!

RANDOM THOUGHT THAT HAPPENS TO BE TRUE

In all areas of your life you are the problem and you are the solution.

Your brain and body are both working overtime during your teenage years. It's worth knowing what's cracking off as, that way, you can do something about it.

In your younger years you go through four phases of development. From zero to two you were 'self-centred'. Everything revolved around you and you never considered anyone else's needs. This is the unconditional you, the blank slate or what Buddhists would call your 'original face'. You were just being you. There was no pretence, no shame, no trying to impress. Let's face it, gurgling with pleasure as your mum whips your nappy off and wipes the poo off your legs is far from impressive. And you didn't even care!

You didn't know if you were male or female, black or white. You weren't fussed about religion and you didn't know school even existed. *Happy days!* You experienced the world, eating it, smelling it, sticking your fingers in places they weren't meant to be, exploring, curious ... your brain was a jello of connectivity.

your 'Original face'

From 3 to 12 you became 'adult-centred'. Mum, dad, gran, they were like Gods. You hugged them. You worshipped them. Your brain created a stupid amount of connections, in fact so many that some had to be trimmed back. So, between 3 and 12, any connections in the brain that weren't being used were pruned back.

The day you hit 13, it all changed again. Okay, not exactly on 13, but some time around then. The 'learned self' started to creep in. You became what boffins call 'peer-group centred'. It's common across all primates. There comes a point where your brain is sufficiently advanced to start thinking and reasoning for yourself. You start to question authority. Family rules might seem trivial and petty. You kick back, push the boundaries and develop your own views and ideas about how the world works. Often, the teenager starts to develop stronger links outside of the family. In monkey terms, you join a troop. In human terms, it's likely to be a handful of besties, maybe even a gang. Fitting into this peer group becomes all important so you dress the same, talk the same, behave the same. You experience an overwhelming desire to fit in. As a result, family can become very uncool so your dad, whom you worshipped last year, is now a bit of an embarrassment. In fact, your desire to fit into a peer group is so strong that it causes a whole lot of anguish if you're excluded. Some research suggests this distress at not fitting in causes more discomfort than physical pain.

There's evidence that teenagers experience more intense emotions than adults, reporting feelings of anxiety and embarrassment three times more than parents. Teenagers also report feeling bored, tired and drowsy. In spite of your youthful body and less harried life, you also experience massive lapses in energy. You have higher highs and lower lows.

Developments between your ears are changing how you experience the world. You develop critical reasoning skills that heighten your sensitivity to life. These advanced reasoning skills allow you, for the first time, to see beneath the surface of situations and imagine hidden threats to your wellbeing. In simple English, you begin to imagine what others think about you.

Cast your mind back, when you were 3 years old you wandered about on the beach, naked, letting it all hang out. You didn't care. Doing that at 14 is a different matter because you've become more sensitive to how others perceive you. There's some evidence that self-consciousness is particularly heightened for teenage girls.

It's a bit of a minefield. Heightened sensitivity is a breeding ground for psychological problems, hence why people turn to drugs, alcohol, self-harm, eating disorders or simply locking themselves away from the world which, in itself, can lead to loneliness and depression.

Holy cow! This is grim stuff. We're telling you so you're aware. For the record, most young people pass through this phase just fine and dandy.

A few can become desperate in dealing with feelings they cannot control (or are too young to know how to control). These feelings can affect families. We're realists. You can't stop growing up, it's kind of inevitable. But you can learn how to cope with it and minimize the negative effects.

Activity: rolling with the punches

As a teenager, you can become hyper-sensitive to what others say about you. Sometimes it's the smallest things that end up upsetting you. To help you roll with the punches, here's a super-cool activity …

Criticism can sting. And there are plenty of people who stand on the edges of life, throwing criticism around. Social media makes this ever so easy.

The trick is to ignore the criticism, unless it's delivered by someone you truly respect and care for. And who cares for you too. In which case the criticism will be well intended.

From now on, the only criticism that you will accept is that delivered by those you respect and/or those whose opinion you value. Think about that inner circle of people – there won't be many. You should be able to write their names in the small box.

Next time someone says something bad, cruel or upsetting, check if their name is in the box. If not, you can ignore the comment because their opinion doesn't count. If their name is in the box, act on their words. They care about you so take measures to improve yourself.

People whose opinions I value ...

Good news. From late-teens onwards, things settle down. The metamorphosis to adulthood smooths you out and, with a bit of luck and some supportive parenting, you turn out alright.

In fact, someone loves you enough to give you this book, so you'll turn out a darn sight better than alright. One day, around your mid-20s, you emerge fully-brained, blinking into the sunlit uplands of the adult world. You've arrived! When you get there, remember to come back to this page and re-read this bit ... *mid-20s, your unique brain is solidified and fully developed and from now on you're much better devoting time to working out what you have and how to make the best of it, rather than trying to change it.*

We were kind of tempted to repeat that sentence for effect, but hope that bold italics will do the trick?

> ## NOW'T BUT THE TRUTH
>
> 'Everyone is screwed up, broken, clingy and scared, even the people who seem to have it most together.'
>
> Anne Lamott (author, mother and grandmother)

Who wants to be a millionaire?

Here's a beautiful new word for you: *Sonder*. You know that craziness in your head? The whirring of thoughts and insecurities? Sonder is the realization that each random passer-by is living a life as vivid and complex as your own–populated with their own ambitions, friends, routines, worries and inherited craziness.

Yes, everyone else is insecure too. Everyone's filled with self-doubt, even the ones who look like they've got their life together. So chill; we're all a little bit crazy!

There will be hundreds of times when you're pushed right out of your comfort zone and you're flailing around in the unknown, not knowing how to behave or react. In an ideal world, we want you to embrace the unknown and go for it. If you can re-programme your inner-voice so that when a challenge arises you say 'Bring it on', then you'll achieve magnificent things in your life.

School, if you play it right that is, will prepare you for exactly that. Instead of bleating 'Why me?' try a bold exclamation of 'What's next?'

Activity: Be teachable

We're going to give you four simple statements. Without over-thinking them, scribble the answers in the spaces below. Not smart-arse answers, truthful ones:

Be the kind of learner your teacher wants you to be, which is …

Three things I can do to make my teacher go 'wow':

Three things I can do, today, that will make my family go 'wow':

What's stopping you doing the things above?

Before we change subject, a quick word about sleep. As a teenager, your body and brain are both going through a metamorphosis, from child to adult. It's a bit like a Dr Who regeneration, but on a slower scale. Your body is working extra hard to regenerate, hence why you're tired. We're not wanting to nag but it's not very clever to deprive yourself of sleep, or to be up late playing games or

makes sense to MAKE a priority

texting, or waking up and checking your phone. You need between eight and ten hours' sleep a night.

Fact!

Let's keep it deadly simple. You've got to get up at 7am to be dressed, breakfasted and off to school. You can struggle out of bed, all groggy and grumbly about it being too early. You can slump to school tired and groggy. Loads of teenagers do.

But actually it's not 'too early', it's time to get up. The secret is, of course, to go to bed a bit earlier. I mean, come on, it's the simplest solution in the entire book. A bedroom's called a BEDroom for a reason. Get the TV, games console and phone out of it.

Remember, your brain is developing like crazy. You're asking a lot of it. Give it a break! Night time is an opportunity for it to go to work, re-wiring, upgrading and rebooting. Give your brain and body a fair chance by getting into good sleep habits.

If the reasoning above doesn't cut the mustard then this should tip the balance in the favour of getting to bed earlier and with no distractions. A British uni did a sleep study and calculated that getting into good sleep habits (i.e., doing our obvious advice above) is equivalent to winning £200,000 a year on the lottery. Every year!

Dear reader, what if your health was the only true wealth? And what if sleep was an important part of the health equation?

Treat yourself to a cheeky little lottery win.

The Money Monster

Grab a pencil. It's thinking time.

Activity: Off the top of your head ...

Complete the next few sentences, there's no right or wrong. The aim is to begin to unearth your core beliefs and values:

People are ...

Happiness is ...

Love means ...

Money is ...

School is …

Friendship is …

Family is …

Success is …

It's interesting to reflect on your answers above, particularly the last one. What, for you, is success?

Lots of money, a nice house, cool job, big car, YouTuber with 10 million followers, footballer, rock star? In the span of your 4000 weeks, how will you know you've achieved 'success'?

Brace yourself for some more grown-up stuff. Your thinking is half right. Money is good, as in it's useful and it can bring you a sense of comfort and ease. It's nice to be able to afford a decent house with enough left over to stick the heating on. Nicer still if there's a cool car on the driveway. Money and stuff isn't going to make you unhappy.

However, that's not quite the end of the money story. Let's nip across to Sweden, one of the happiest countries on the planet. Maybe it's because they have six months of summer when the sun never sets, or it could be that their happiness is piqued by their liking

it's NOT gonna make you happy!!!

for mixed-gender naked saunas. That would be a dreadful stereotype, so instead, let's introduce you to a Swedish concept, *lagom*, a word that has no direct English translation. The best we can give you is 'sufficiency' or 'enoughness'.

Here's how the world works. Big companies spend billions on marketing, so they produce sexy adverts and glossy posters that make you drool over their product. You end up musterbating – let me clarify – 'musterbation' is when you turn things you'd like to have into things you think you MUST have. The end result is that you have to buy that product and then you'll be happy. So you do, and you are. For a day or two. And then you see someone with a better phone, tablet, shoes, jeans than you ... and you start musterbating again.

Purchasing things to make you happy is like putting an Elastoplast on a severed leg.

Back to *lagom* – learning to be satisfied with what you already have is a pretty cool happiness trick. The world is a bit like an all-you-can-eat buffet, with everything spread out before you. It's less about knowing where to start, and more about knowing when to stop.

Activity: Lucky you

Try this for size. Write a list of 30 things you're lucky to have but take for granted:

01.	07.
02.	08.
03.	09.
04.	10.
05.	11.
06.	12.

13.	**22.**
14.	**23.**
15.	**24.**
16.	**25.**
17.	**26.**
18.	**27.**
19.	**28.**
20.	**29.**
21.	**30.**

Please note, we're not saying 'stuff' is bad, or that money is the root of all evil. Stuff is great. And money is lush. Our point is much more subtle. Stuff and money won't make you unhappy, but the *relentless pursuit of more* will.

Please note, this is a very grown-up point that most grown-ups don't get. Look around you and you'll see hordes of people traipsing through life in the relentless pursuit of more. Bored people binging on Netflix, fat folk stuffing their faces at Dominos, teenagers chasing a phone upgrade. *More, more, more!* If you don't believe me, poke your head into your mum's wardrobe and count the number of pairs of shoes. Ask, *'Mum, why do you have 53 pairs of shoes and 18 handbags?'* and see what she says.

Then explain *lagom* to her.

Have a look at your list above. Look at what you've already got and rejoice. Compared with your ancestors who had nothing, you are rich beyond imagination.

Sticking with the richness theme, it's interesting that if you ask, *'Who wants to be a millionaire?'* to an assembly hall of children, 100% will enthusiastically raise their hands, whereas about half will raise their hands to *'Who wants to be happy?'*

So, to challenge your thinking, let's change the question to something much more interesting: *What would you rather have, '£1m' or 'not be dead'?*

It might take a nano-second but most people will instinctively go for option 2. In fact, I can probably raise the stakes and offer you £10m and you'd still opt for the alive option?

Is this some stupid play on words, a silly mind game, or simply a reminder of the value you place on life? It seems that most people merely forget how awesome being alive is so consider this chapter as a massive reminder. You're here, reading these words. Therefore you're alive, you're educated and that's a decent starting point because we've already worked out that it's worth a million quid to you. We're not suggesting you dress like a tramp and make do with the worst mobile phone ever. More that there's a big fat chance that you already have enough.

Understanding *lagom* and learning to curb your materialistic desires is a much bigger happiness factor than you imagine.

Oh, and a final word on quitting the materialistic arms race – waiting for everybody else to change is pointless. You'll die waiting. Be grateful, starting now. We dare you to be happy with what you've already got.

Holiday Offer

Let's make you an offer – not just a holiday – the adventure of a lifetime!

Imagine, just for a moment, that we've invited you on an amazing trip into the solar system. We're going to spend the next 90 years cruising amongst the stars.

In fact, let's upgrade the trip ... let's go the long way and journey around the sun. The holiday is free and, in true game-show style, I'll throw in some spending money.

The big question is: would you go?

Ninety years is a long time, right? You're thinking that you'd miss your family, friends and cat. So let's upgrade you further. So you're not lonely, you can take all your family and friends. Your cat/dog/guinea pig. Your house and, the clincher, I'll give you Wi-Fi.

You're probably thinking, there's a catch? You can't possibly be offering a lifetime of space travel, with family and friends. With Wi-Fi! For FREE?

And, yes there is a catch. Welcome to Earth. This is the journey you are already on. Your home is a ball of rock, spinning on its axis as it hurtles through space at 67,000 mph (thanks Wiki). Around us are billions of other lumps of rock. Earth travels all the way around the sun every single year. You already have friends, family and Wi-Fi. Maybe even some spending money too?

Part 3

BRILLIANT FUTURE

Prepare yourself for some animal magic – this chapter contains eagles, crocs (the reptile, not the fashion failure), dolphins, Bambi, pigeons and elephants.

But mostly it's about the day the circus came to town and the importance of developing a backbone instead of a wishbone. We also squeeze in a section about why human beings are pre-programmed for danger and the importance of getting top quality ingredients into a sausage machine.

We reveal the success formula, in which effort counts twice, and look at things that are worth giving up. Indeed, giving up is often the secret of moving forward. We ask whether you want an easy life or a good life, arguing that people who live within their comfort zones might actually be very uncomfortable.

Then it's onto goal setting, via icebergs and the spag bol of success. We introduce Everest Goals that can turn dreams into reality and finish with a couple of celebs: a scientific one and an Olympic one. Usain Bolt, quadruple gold medallist and the fastest human being ever – what a loser! (At badminton, that is.)

Confused? Let's hope so. Off we trot ...

Eagles, Dolphins, Crocs and You

In the book that keeps giving, here's another science gem. When a rocket launches, it uses 90% of its fuel to get off the ground. So there's a massive effort in getting started. Once it's done the first half mile, things get easier and once it's in space, it shoots forward almost effortlessly.

So here it is, the third part of our four-parter. If you've got this far you'll have sussed that none of this is rocket science. But this section should act like rocket fuel.

Hang onto your pants, you have lift-off ...

SIMPLEST TOP TIP EVS?

Be teachable.

It's easy to whinge and, yes, it's tough being a teenager in the modern world. But not as tough as being a baby eagle. They learn to fly by being pushed out of the nest. Imagine? Mum gives them a nudge and yikes, they have 500 feet to learn!

Slow learner? SPLAT!

Dolphins are born swimming. Turtles are born with an instinct to run to the sea as fast as their flippers will take them. If you watch the veterinary programmes, a calf is born, mum gives it a bit of a lick clean and it's on its wobbly legs within an hour. Ditto Bambi. Most animals are born world-ready.

We are not 'most animals'. When you were new-born, people ran around after you. You couldn't talk but you were a surprisingly good communicator, with a cry for every occasion: *'I want booby milk, yes at 2am', 'I'm too hot', 'I've pooped, yet again'*. But babies are rubbish at everything else.

Why?

Compared to other primates human babies are born too early for their brain to be fully developed. Your mum would have needed you in her tum for two years if you were to emerge fully brained. We pop out at nine months because our heads won't fit through that tiny escape hatch. If we stayed in there any longer, your mum would probably never walk again. So, head-size is a problem that evolution has solved by birthing our offspring before they're properly ready. The bun in the oven comes out before it's properly baked.

Your brain is the most complex thing in the universe so let's dumb it down using 'old' and 'new'. The old part of your brain doesn't think, it just reacts. It dates back a few million years and is rather like a lizard's brain. Exactly in fact. And, boy, is it quick. The old part acts faster than you can think. Put your hand on a hotplate and you'll see what I mean – there's no *'Mmm, what's that burning smell?'*; the lizard brain acts at supersonic speed.

A few hundred thousand years ago, humans developed a new part of the brain, the neo-cortex, that's the bit above your eyebrows. This serves two incredibly useful purposes: firstly, it allows you to keep your hat on and, secondly, it's your thinking brain. This relatively new bolt-on is what distinguishes us from, say, pigeons (that and their ability to fly, and feathers and a few other bits and bobs).

This new bit is slower than the old part, but it allows humans to rationalize, ponder, imagine, reflect, worry, sulk and empathize. Pigeons tend not to worry about homework, Instagram or whether their bum looks big.

This new bit is fab, but there's a design fault. When we look around at our fabulous lives, it's easy to forget that our ancestors eked out a meagre existence. They lived in small groups. It was very uncommon to meet someone you didn't know and often dangerous when you did. Couple that with starvation, parasites, injury, no prescription drugs, no police – the world really was a dangerous place. The human brain was moulded by the need to survive and reproduce. It evolved with a hair-trigger readiness to react to danger. In fact, from a survival standpoint, if you failed to heed danger there would be no tomorrow.

For example, your *great great great great great great great great great great* grandpa could make two kinds of mistakes: first, thinking there was a snake in the bushes when there wasn't one, and second, thinking there was no snake in the bushes when there actually was one. The cost of the first mistake was a pounding heart and needless anxiety. The cost of the second one was death. Consequently, we evolved to make the first mistake a million times to avoid making the second one even once.

Cut to today and the dangers have receded but the same brain circuitry is continually scanning for danger. This is just the way it is. It's not just you, it's the human race. It's called 'negativity bias' and it's always lurking in the background. Negativity bias tilts your world towards immediate survival, but away from happiness, peace, contentment and joy.

It's why negative news gets reported and spread so much more readily. It's why we can't turn away from a car accident or two people fighting. It's why it's so much more tempting to relate to others through complaining and gossip rather than through gratitude. It's why you notice the one negative remark said about you, and delete the 100 positives. It's why one bad moment can ruin your day.

HEAD SPACE

'Don't let negative and toxic people rent space in your head. Raise the rent and kick them out.'

Robert Tew (famous dancer)

That means you have to re-train your brain to notice the positives.

So here's a really cool tried and tested activity that will help you tune into positivity and, crucially, will gradually reshape your brain and begin to tilt it towards happiness and gratitude.

Activity: Three good things

For the next week we want you to reflect on three good things that have happened, or three good things that you've noticed. They don't have to be massive events, but we want you to take a few minutes at the end of each day to make a few notes. For example, they can be events, such as *'I put my hand up in class today, and got an answer right'* or simple moments like *'I noticed the lovely blue sky today'*. Record the activity and the feeling in the spaces below:

Day 1	
Three good things	My feelings
1	
2	
3	

Day 2	
Three good things	My feelings
1	
2	
3	

Day 3	
Three good things 1 2 3	My feelings

Day 4	
Three good things 1 2 3	My feelings

Day 5	
Three good things 1 2 3	My feelings

Day 6	
Three good things 1 2 3	My feelings
Day 7	
Three good things 1 2 3	My feelings

Top tip

Conventional wisdom suggests that, if you're angry, you should 'count to ten', which allows the red mist to evaporate.

Research suggests that, once the source of anger is removed, your emotion system returns to normal after about 20 minutes. So, here's a tip: don't count to ten when you're mad, count to 1,200!

An even better top tip is to learn to stay calm and not get angry in the first place.

Sausages

As a baby, people ran around after you, and you kind of liked it. In fact, you got used to it. Now you're older, people will still be running around after you, cooking your meals, dropping you off at school, paying for your phone, etc.

This is an interesting time for you because you'll be going through a big transition. Not just in terms of your body sprouting extra parts and hairy bits, or riding an emotional ghost train as your hormones settle into place. Nope. Something much bigger than that. From mid to late teenage-hood, people will stop treating you like a child. The bad news is that you have to stop acting like one. You have to stop expecting your mum to cook, clean and fuss after you, and start mucking in, looking after yourself.

Your parents and teachers will call it 'taking personal responsibility for your life'. We have a technical term for the same thing; we call it *growing up*. Everyone has to do it. The onus is on you to make it as painless as possible, for yourself and those around you.

HOW THE WORLD WORKS

Nobody thinks they're stupid. That's part of the stupidity.

Richard Wilkins likens life to a sausage machine. Use your vivid teenage imagination and imagine such a contraption.

You know the routine – the ingredients go in at one end, you turn a handle and an endless string of sausages is squeezed out of the other end. If you wanted pork sausages you'd stick a squealing piggy in at the ingredients end. If you wanted vegetarian sausages, you'd put squealing vegetarians in. Without insulting your intelligence, if you wanted Quorn sausages, you wouldn't stick a horse in. It just doesn't work like that.

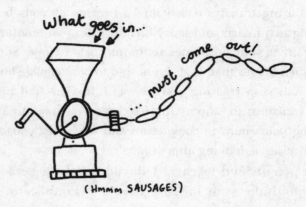

what goes in...

...must come out!

(Hmmm SAUSAGES)

And then there's life itself. Imagine the same sausage machine principle, but instead of sausages, it's now your life, the precious 4000 weeks that you've been granted. Same routine, so you stuff the ingredients of life in at one end, turn the handle and your life is squeezed out of the other end. Keep turning the handle and day after day spews out, pretty much like the chain of sausages from the previous paragraph.

Look, you've got this far, so we're going to treat you with a degree of intelligence way beyond your years. If you wanted your life to be, say, 'confident' and 'positive', what ingredients would you need to put in? (Remember, pork in/pork out, veggies in/veggies out.)

The truth about growing up is that it's your life, it's your 4000 weeks, and therefore they're your ingredients. You can put whatever you want into the sausage machine of life. Here's an experiment you should try. For the next two days, put 'can't be bothered', 'negativity', 'grumbling' and 'nightmare' into your life and see what happens. Then, for the two days after that, stick 'positivity', 'confidence', 'happiness' and 'hard work' into your sausage machine.

Monitor the results. How do you feel? How much energy do you have? What are you like to be around? What results are you getting?

If the first two days of negativity get you the perfect result, go with those. If the awesome ingredients win, go with those.

The law of the sausage machine says it's up to you. Your choice! #Simples

The Effort Formula

The message from Part 1, butchered to one sentence is something like this: *Start where you are with what you have.* If we stretched to two sentences we might add, *and what you have is plenty.* A third would be, *it takes effort to be your best self.*

So, picking up from there, let's explore why you should be bothered. The 'e' word – *effort* – is a bit off-putting. Your argument could be '*Why bother to put in extra effort over and above what everyone else is doing?*'

First up, it doesn't matter what everyone else is doing. We're not talking about *their* 4000 weeks and *their* potential, we're talking about *yours*. Therefore, it matters what *you* are doing.

The iceberg picture reveals the secret of success. For everyone. Ever.

ALMOST POETIC

'Most of the shadows of this life are caused by our standing in our own sunshine.'

Ralph Waldo Emerson (American guy who wrote essays for a living. Imagine!)

We hang around in the adult world and, let's be blunt, most people live well within their limits. There seems little point in being energized below your maximum and behaving below your optimum. It's like driving a Lamborghini at 27mph. Or worse, it's like being in possession of a whole load of superpowers that you fail to use. I mean, who would you rather be, Peter Parker or Spidey; Diana or Wonder Woman?

You may not even know you have superpowers? They can be heavily disguised: musical, sporting, academic, dance, art, bricklaying, history, numbers, writing, cooking, kindness, positivity, making people laugh, YouTubing, listening, public speaking, coding, acting, organizing, science, teaching, caring, fixing, inventing, figuring things out, acting, technology, imagineering ... any of these abilities will enable you to make money. But only if you discover them and bring them to life.

MORE DARN TRUTH!

'We all love to win, but how many people love training?'

Mark Spitz (multi-gold Olympic swimmer)

Activity

Write down a list of people you admire. People who've achieved things. Your heroes ...

1.

2.

3.

4.

5.

We're pretty sure your list will consist of talented people – actors, pop stars, sporting legends – that kind of thing. The modern world promotes the cult of genius. We are conned into thinking genius is something magical. It's a huge get-out clause which tells us that we're not obliged to compare ourselves with geniuses because they were born that way.

Were they? *Really?*

Or was there some seriously hard graft involved?

There's some smart research that says talent is important but effort counts twice. Keeping it simple, how do you become really skilful at anything? Netball, baking, painting your nails, art, gaming, building websites, pottery, tennis, maths, football, YouTubing …

$$\text{Skill} = \text{Talent} \times \text{Effort}$$

When you consider individuals in identical circumstances, what each achieves depends on just two things: talent and effort. Talent relates to how fast we can improve in skill. Let's apply it to a subject, say tennis. A little bit of talent is useful, but talent without effort means you'll never get skilful.

That's part one. Once you've got skilful, ask yourself what makes the breakthrough to achievement?

$$\text{Achievement} = \text{Skill} \times \text{Effort}$$

So hang on, effort figures again? *Absolutely!*

Effort counts twice. You won't acquire skill without it, and you won't achieve without putting effort into honing your skills.

At this point, you have choices about the internal voice. It can go all shouty: *'Oh my gosh! That's the worst dirty little secret in the whole damn book! You've basically lulled me into reading a book in which the top 'top tip' is exactly the same top tip that my teachers and parents have been telling me, right from age 10. Try my bestest! Is that it? It's a con. It's soooo unfair! Where's my phone? I need to tell the world that I've been violated ...'*

The paragraph above is what the old version of you would have thought. You'd have gone into meltdown mode, all stereotypically eye-rolly, histrionic and snowflaky. But we've given you so much info and priming that by now, your reaction will be different. Hopefully something akin to *'Effort counts twice? In-ter-esting.* (You have to say that like a movie baddie, ideally with one eyebrow raised.) *It kind of hangs with the rest of the messages in the book – common sense but not common practice. Stuff I already knew but was making excuses not to do. Know what, if effort really does count twice, I may as well up my game. Thanks authors, I'm gonna go onto Amazon, right now, and give this book a 5* review ...'*

Effort counts twice? Oscar-nominated actor Will Smith once said it on a chat show better than us: 'I've never really viewed myself as particularly talented ... where I excel is ridiculous, sickening work ethic.' He goes on, 'I will not be outworked. You might have more talent than me, be smarter than me, you might be sexier than me. You might be all of those things. You got me in nine categories. But if we get on the treadmill together, there's two things. You're getting off first, or I'm gonna die. It's really that simple.'

GODDAMMIT, MORE TRUTH!

Enthusiasm is common. Endurance is rare.

Re-dreaming Your Dream

Let's apply the effort formula to me. When I was age 15. Like a lot of teenage lads, I wanted to be a footballer. So I trained quite hard and got pretty good.

But here's the rub. There's a chasm between being 'pretty good' and being 'extraordinary' and the only way to close that gap is to go for it in a big way. That meant maximum mental and physical effort, healthy eating and an ultra-positive mindset. Hindsight has taught me that I was in love with the image, the stadium, the cheering, the medals, the England caps, the fame, the cars, the cash and the WAGs, but I wasn't in love with the process.

I tried, quite hard. I made the effort to get skilful. But I also tried hard at drinking beer and going to parties. Then I got a bad injury and coming back from that was going to be seriously hard work. This was where I needed to kick on, the part of the equation where I applied myself and turned my skill into achievement. Sadly, this was a push too far. I wanted the reward but not the struggle. I was in love with the victory but not the fight. There were easier and quicker ways to happiness. Short-term happiness that is.

It's easy to look back and see where it all fell apart. I had let go of long-term happiness in favour of the easy-peasy 'now' variety. Boy, those teenage parties were good.

They also killed my dream.

Delving (yet again) into deep stuff that most books don't tell you, at the core of all human behaviour, most people's needs are more or less similar. We want more positive experiences because they make us feel good and they're easy to handle. It's negative experiences that we all struggle with. Therefore, what we get out of life is not determined purely by the good feelings we desire but by what bad feelings we're willing and able to sustain to get us to those good feelings.

For example, if you want to lose a bit of weight, you know that you will have to burn off more calories than you consume. That's pretty much the only way it works. So, yes, you want to lose weight but not if you have to stop eating cake. Or go to the gym. Or, heaven forbid, both! So, you wanting to achieve your goal weighs less than your desire for an easy life. Similarly, you want to do really well in your exams but that means working hard in class, plus long hours of study in your own time.

So, counter-intuitively, the question may be less about what you want to achieve and more like *'What pain are you willing to sustain to achieve it?'* Paradoxically, what if the quality of your life is not determined by the quality of your positive experiences but your willingness to tolerate negative experiences?

That dear reader is a remarkably big thought. So in the interests of challenging you, it's worth pondering what your three big goals might be, and what you're willing to *give up* to achieve them.

Activity: What am I willing to sacrifice?

We're asking you for three things you want to achieve: one at school, one outside of school and one random exciting goal:

#1 Big thing I want to achieve at school

What I'm willing to *give up* to achieve it

#1 Big thing I want to achieve outside of school

What I'm willing to *give up* to achieve it

#1 other big thing that I want to achieve

What I'm willing to *give up* to achieve it

INTERESTING NOTION

'If you're caught in a trap, what's the one thing you have to do before you can escape? You have to realize that you've been caught in a trap!'

Jamie Smart (Brit, writer and modern-day philosopher)

Deep down, we know we want more out of life than Netflix and Instagram. I got sick to death of strolling along the path of least resistance, aka walking in the lazy lane. It's as though my dreams were way over there somewhere, waving to me. *CooEee. Hello there. I'm the awesome grades you could have if you pulled your finger out.*

Yeah. Whatever. It was easier to coast, and then get home and veg out on Netflix and fast food.

You want easy? Here's easy ...

- It's effortless to fit into doing what everyone else is doing, namely being self-critical and sinking into negative conversations.

- Playing thousands of hours on a computer game is a whole lot easier than spending thousands of hours learning coding and writing a computer game.

- Lounging in bed for an extra hour takes way less effort than getting up and exercising.

- Watching a talent show on TV is much simpler than learning to play the guitar and going on a talent show.

- Coasting through a history module is a doddle compared to applying yourself and learning loads.

- Getting to the end of your 4000 weeks having achieved about 25% of your potential is a snip compared to the effort of getting to the end and going *'Wow, that was amazing!'*

Basically, we're drawn to things that are easy and convenient.

I think I'll just sit here and wait for my life to get better.

Hellooooo! Wakey-wakey!

Our message is to do what's best, not what's easiest. Life's journey is not to arrive at the grave safely in a well preserved body, but rather to skid in sideways, totally worn out, shouting *'Holy moley ... what a ride!'*

Success is Like a Plate of Spag

Your teachers care. Yes, yes, I know you will be able to think of an exception, but on the whole, they care and they care a lot. Not just about your grades either. Here's something you've never considered, and that's absolutely true, it really hurts them when you don't care back.

The school system is there to help you. You're supported.

A BIG FAT LIKELIHOOD

Your teachers believe in you more than you believe in you.

Guess what, as soon as you leave school, people stop caring. It's baby eagle time! You've got a lot of learning to do, and quick!

Success does not happen in a straight line, it's like a plate of spaghetti. Not just in that it's a tangle, but also that it's slippery and messy.

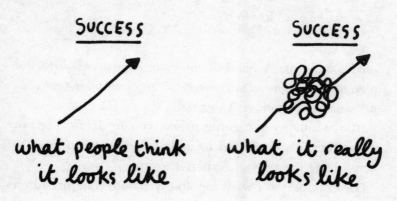

SUCCESS

SUCCESS

what people think
it looks like

what it really
looks like

But before we talk about success, let's flip the coin to failure. A lot of the clichés fall flat on their face if you do them to death. We get the symbolism of *'quitters never quit'* or that *'failure is not an option'*, but, in reality, they do and it is! Failure is a big fat option but then, so is success. If you have the courage to consistently push for success you have to accept that there are times when you'll lose.

Failure doesn't have to put you back on the naughty step. Get your backside on the positive step. What have you just learned? What will you do differently next time? How can this failure move you forward?

Top tip

Always focus on want you want to achieve, rather than what you want to avoid.

Nobody wants to fail. I doubt anyone relishes failure. But in another of those bizarre twists of logic, willingness to fail increases your chances of success.

In a minute, we're going to ask you to dream big but before that, it's important to understand that you need to focus on the *process* rather than the *result*.

For example, you want fabulously mouth-watering exam results that stick a middle finger up to your teacher – you need to focus (and I mean *really focus*) on the process. You can't just wish for stellar exam results. The process will be something that starts with a realization that exams aren't really at the end of your school year. Exams start NOW. The 'process' involves a great deal of hard work, NOW. So extra reading, making some notes from your books, researching some YouTube vids on the subject, doing top secret extra work that nobody knows about. *Now!*

Glamorous? *Nope.*

And remember, there's stuff that you will have to sacrifice to achieve stellar results. But while the rest of the teenagers are Instagramming pictures of cats and/or marauding through a computer game, you'll be inching ahead. Bit by bit, these extras build into a significant advantage. It's effort rearing its ugly-mugly head again!

Being consistently motivated means you have to dig deep and it can be a lonely activity. Teachers will be doing everything they can, but they can't do it for you. And we come full circle, back to your inner story. It's easy to listen to the story that goes *'I'm not that bothered anyway'*. It's much harder to craft a story in which you're the hard-working superhero that makes your parents and teachers proud.

A POULTRY THOUGHT

Inside every turkey there's a wishbone. But to get it, the turkey has to be murdered, plucked, stuffed and cooked – none of which were on the turkey's wish list.

It's true that laziness pays off now whereas hard work pays off in the future. You cannot achieve your ambitions just by wishing, otherwise everyone who had a wish would be living their dream life. And boy oh boy, looking around the adult world, most people certainly are not!

But hang in there, the soup is about to get a whole lot thicker. Hard work is a vital ingredient, but there are two others which we'll visit via the circus and Everest ...

What Has the Circus Ever Done for Me?

Here's a true story. When I was 11, the circus came to town. Obviously, I'm ancient now so this was back in the day when circuses had animals, and this particular circus had an elephant. Just the one. Unimaginatively, he was called Dumbo, and he was the main attraction, so much so that he stood outside the big top and, as we arrived, my sister and I got to join the queue of excited children and we patted Dumbo and fed him a bun. I'm assuming that someone had done a risk assessment on Dumbo? He was a wild animal after all and if he got spooked, a stampeding elephant could have caused havoc. So Dumbo had a rope tied around one of his ankles, with the other end of the rope tied to a tent peg that had been hammered into the turf.

Let's replay that scene one more time, just so it's clear in your mind. We have a three-ton wild animal, with a flimsy rope around its ankle, tied to a tent peg that has been hammered into the soft grass.

Are you thinking what I'm thinking?

Why did Dumbo not think ... *wild animal ... three tons ... tent peg* ... yank his leg free and stampede to the croissant and pastries aisle at Sainsbury's. Why on earth did Dumbo stand there and accept his fate?

Well, it could partly be that he was being fed sticky buns, so was perfectly content in the moment. It's a whole lot easier to stand there and accept your fate. But I suspect it was almost entirely due to his thinking. You see, when Dumbo was a baby elephant he'd been chained to a lamp post, with no means of escape. He'd tugged and tugged at the chain and all he got was a bleeding and swollen ankle. So when Dumbo had grown up, the tent peg was enough to hold him. He'd stopped trying. The rope wasn't really holding him back, his thinking most definitely was. Dumbo had developed what scientists would call 'learned helplessness'. The three-ton wild beast had simply forgotten.

It's hard for this next sentence to sound anything other than harsh, but, *are you that elephant?* Are there things in your head that are holding you back? Is your thinking limiting your potential?

Are YOU the biggest thing that stands between you and your dreams?

Hugging

A FOCUSING THOUGHT

You are always focused. You never ever lose focus. But sometimes you might focus on the wrong things.

If you want to be truly world class, we advocate that you take a bit of a gamble, go against the tide of traditional thinking and set massive goals. We call them Huge Unbelievably Great Goals, or HUGGS. A HUGG is something that is currently out of reach – you have to grow, innovate and engage in order to achieve it. A HUGG is on the edges of achievability but it's not out of sight. It might be that you only get half way there – but your achievements will reach far beyond having no HUGG at all. A HUGG isn't something to be afraid of – it's something to aspire to.

Maybe a better name would be 'Everest goals'? Has Mount Everest ever been conquered? *Yup*. But only by a committed few.

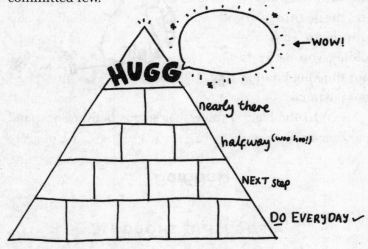

IN IT TO WIN IT

Interviewer to Jamie Vardy: …'You've got a 5000–1 chance of winning the league.'
Vardy: *'So we've got a chance.'*

Jamie Vardy (Stocksbridge Park Steels footballer who somehow ended up winning the Premier League with 5000-1 shot, Leicester City)

Stretching yourself is good. But to maintain your motivation you need to know where you're stretching to. You need a goal, a mouth-wateringly exciting thing to aim for, and that's where our HUGG pyramid comes into being.

Rewind. A few years ago I went on a training course run by an heroic genius called David Hyner and he introduced me to HUGGs. So I got home and did one. At that time I had an idea swirling in my head about a children's book based on my pet dog. What if while I was at work and my kids were at school, my mutt went around town catching baddies and solving crimes? What if she was a secret agent, a bit like James Bond but a dog, undercover as an ordinary family pet. What if she was a Spy Dog?

A million 'Spy Dog' book sales later, I'm telling you, this HUGG thing works. Next, I decided to achieve something that nobody had ever done before; I was going to become a Doctor of Happiness. That job actually didn't even exist when I decided to do it.

And yet, 12 years and a lot of hard work later, I am now it!

The trick is to write your *Huge Unbelievable Great Goal* in the bubble at the top of the pyramid and to make it compelling. That means not only is it a big ambition, but that you really want it. It has to excite you. And when you've written it, stop and have a think. Chances are, you can write it better. So, for example, *'To go to uni'* is fine, but *'To go to a top 10 university'* is finer. *'To be a doctor'* is nice. *'To be the best doctor in my hospital'* is nicer. *'To be a hairdresser'* is all well and good, but *'To own and run a chain of the world's most amazing beauty salons'* is weller and gooder.

Got it? Good. Pen at the ready ...

Activity: Turning goals into HUGGs

In which case, re-write these piffling goals into Huge Unbelievably Great Goals:

To pass my GCSEs

To do well in my A-levels

To get a part in the school play

To join the army

To be a gamer

To be a footballer

To be an actress

We're hoping that you'll 'get' that to *be an OSCAR-winning actress* elevates the goal to a HUGG. As does, to *smash my A-levels and get into a top 10 uni*. Or to *get one of the lead parts in my school play.*

Once you've nailed what your huge goal is, you then start at the bottom of the pyramid and work out what you've got to start doing EVERY SINGLE DAY OF YOUR LIFE – to stand any chance of that goal ever happening. The thing about HUGGs is, of course, that they're jaw-droppingly big. You aren't going to get into a top university by accident. Ditto becoming a Prem footballer, top scientist, #1 YouTuber or A-grade mathser.

Life is a never-ending upward spiral. If you think you're ever allowed to stop climbing, I'm afraid you've missed the point. The joy is in the climb itself. Plain simple English yet again, that means a re-think of your thinking so that when there's a challenge you move away from rolling your eyes and huffing that *'it's not fair'* to a steely-eyed nod of *'bring it on'*.

So, when the bottom row is filled in, you go to the next level of the pyramid. When you've started doing the things on the bottom row, what next? And next? And after that?

When you're finished, you will have a proper HUGG, in all its motivational glory. Stick it on your bedroom wall. It will tell you what the huge goal is, and give you a simple set of things to do or habits to adopt, that will move you forward.

There are no guarantees. You will need some luck along the way.

In fact, let's change the guarantees sentence – there is only one guarantee – your huge goal won't happen by accident. It will only happen if you take sustained action.

And guess what, even if you don't quite achieve your Huge Unbelievably Great Goal, you'll have taken some massive strides forward. You'll be way ahead of the version of you that had no idea what their goal was!

Your Inner Superhero

At a 'celebrity' level, *Time* magazine's 'Person of the 20th Century' would have been consigned to the dustbin of history if we'd focused on his failings. When our celeb was growing up he was referred to as the 'dopey one' and he struggled with words to the point that his family feared he'd never learn to speak. He struggled at school with one teacher telling him he'd never amount to anything and was wasting everyone's time. He muddled through college with uneven grades and struggled to find a job. Our man wanted to be a teacher but it took him fully nine years to land his first teaching job. As if all these weaknesses weren't enough, he was unbelievably absent-minded. Famously, he couldn't remember his own phone number.

This is hardly the stuff of comic books – but of course all we've talked about are his weaknesses. Fortunately, he didn't focus on his weaknesses, but his strengths. Our hero's strength lay in creative thinking – imagining thought experiments that involved theoretical physics. Rather than thinking in words, he thought in pictures. He imagined what things would look like if he were to travel on a bullet at the speed of light and whether space might curve, so the distance between two points is not necessarily a straight line.

With his incredible imagination, he helped to prove the existence of atoms and dreamed up science's most famous equation: $E = MC^2$. With his brilliant thoughts, he revolutionized science.

Of course, we are talking about Albert Einstein, considered by many the greatest genius who ever lived.

So, guess what, Einstein was like you and me – genius at some things and spectacularly bad at others. Fortunately, he worked hard to develop his strengths and didn't let his weaknesses hold him back.

And that's what made him stand head and shoulders above so many others. Sadly, our preoccupation with fixing weaknesses also does a great hatchet job of diminishing the strengths on the other side. It creates a whole load of averageness and means nobody will be outstanding at anything. Eradicating weaknesses creates middling, run-of-the-mill, Jack-of-all-trades.

Activity: Unleashing your inner-strengths

What are you good at?

What are you great at?

What are the things that you find effortless?

What (and/or who) gives you energy?

Reflecting on the questions above, what are your strengths? (If you can't think of any change the question to: *If I asked your best friend, what would they say your strengths are?*)

What do they look like in action?

Give an example of when you used them

How can you use them more?

What would happen if you did?

Exaggerate your strengths and turn yourself into a superhero. Sketch what your strengths look like (i.e., draw a pic of you in action, using your strengths. Pants on the outside? Compulsory!)

Let's update the Einstein example. At the time of writing Usain Bolt holds the world record for being the fastest human being on earth. Google him. Back-to-back Olympic 100m and 200m golds. The man's a machine.

And yet Usain Bolt is spectacularly bad at the 10,000 metres and one of the world's worst marathon runners. You could argue that Usain Bolt is a complete failure! So he did what you should do. Acknowledge what you're rubbish at but focus your life on areas of strength.

Back to the 2%ers again – they aren't trying to be perfect, they have weaknesses, just like everyone else. The key is to focus on honing your strengths and finding ways to play to them.

BRILLIANT MOMENTS

BRILLIANT MOMENTS

And so to Part 4 of our three-parter ... the bonus section, specially concocted for the hard core teenagers who have gotten this far but are still hungry. Part 4 is very moreish – it's the secret sauce on the takeaway of life.

Open your mind to eggs and hatching, then change and transformation, then pineapple chunks and [for the squeamish, please look away now] we ask you to consider that your mum and dad have actually had sex. Hopefully only once, just sufficient to create you. If you can shake that image off, we give you nine things that require no talent.

NINE?

There's no such list as 'nine'. So we ask you to up it to ten, before moving onto to 'super-wellness' via Kung Fu Panda.

You are not a cucumber (phew!) is our way of turning your head inside-out. We introduce you to a basic thinking lesson and then upgrade you to quantum level, way beyond your normal human being.

Have you got a mind full? Or are you mindful? We give you plot twists and finish with a BANG – the Greeks – what have they ever done for us? Yes, okay: olives, feta cheese, they had some philosophers, they invented the Olympics and the marathon. I think they also do a wicked rich, creamy yoghurt. And they might have invented democracy.

But other than all those things?

And that'll take you to the end. Our book ends and your life begins. Your full-colour epic adventure. Make it a thriller.

> **TODAY'S MANTRA:**
>
> I am brilliant, gorgeous, talented and fabulous, *and so is everyone else.*

Okay, here it is. The *fourth* part of the trilogy. The section that only the really committed teenagers reach. Remember, most young people can't be bothered to read a book about personal development. Those who *can* be bothered will get stuck at the earlier sections that mention 'hard work'. They'll have rolled their eyes and gone back to Instagramming pictures of their lunch.

And yet here you are in Part 4. Thanks for hanging in there. Your reward is that we're going to remove the boxing gloves and give you the bare-knuckle truth, the adult stuff that they don't tell you at school or work, but that blows your mind and gives you a MASSIVE advantage over the mortals. Your teachers don't know this stuff, and neither do your ma and pa.

Yes, you wonderful human being, we are here to tell you that you are already a superhero, but it's time to stop pretending to be normal.

Here it is, in a nutshell. Imagine you lived in an egg. A nice cosy, comfortable egg. 'Change' is about staying in your egg. Maybe you can paint your egg so it looks funky and decorate the inside so it's extra comfy and cosy. Change is tinkering with what already is. Note, being busy and being productive are two different things.

There are a lot of people, the tinkers, busy folk, in a perpetual state of change.

Transformation is different. It's about hatching.

This is what our final section is about. There's a whole world out there. A full colour life to be lived. Adventures to be had, laughter lines etched onto your face, experiences to be experienced ... and yet most people stay in their egg.

Flap your wings and get pecking. Let's get cracking [sorry about that] ...

What's the Point of Nine?

Life is a wonderful thing. Mostly. It helps if you've got talent and intelligence – which you have. But even if you think you haven't there aren't any excuses because here are nine things that require no talent or intelligence whatsoever.

1. Being on time. There's a famous saying in Hollywood that 80 per cent of success is turning up. If you can show up in life AND be on time, well that must be more than 80% of your success, in the bag.

2. Being present. Or, as we like to say, if you're in the room, BE in the room. A weird sentence for sure. It's from the same school of thinking that says 'be where your feet are'.

Be present. Be here. Be in the now. When you're scrolling on your phone or when you're playing a computer game you're not in this world. You're lost in another.

3. Work stupidly hard. A toughie. I mean, why should you? It's a lot easier to work reasonably hard or indeed, to do the bare minimum. Check the title of this book before you move on. It's not 'life, the universe and *bog-standardness*'.

Thank you.

4. Body language. More powerful than you will ever imagine – the way you stand, sit, walk, eat – is telling a powerful story about who you are. Everything speaks. By that, we mean that your message is louder than the words you say. How you move and express yourself around others shapes who you are and what they think of you. Don't overdo it, but our advice is to walk tall, sit in class like you're really interested, increase your smileage by 40%, have a teensie bit of a spring in your step (skipping to school and grinning at complete strangers is a sign that you've taken our advice too far).

Seriously, get your body language right and you'll receive a double bonus of a) you'll feel engaged with the world and, b) other people will feel energized around you.

5. Attitude. A positive attitude doesn't cost a bean and it requires absolutely no talent. Yes, there may be a little bit of effort in maintaining an upbeat approach to life but the more you do it, the easier it gets. No one else can decide that. A great attitude maximizes the talent that you do have and offsets what you lack.

6. Being teachable. Costs nothing and requires absolutely no talent. Just good body language, nice manners and your best learning face.

7. Go the extra mile. Exceed your own expectations.

8. Step up. Create opportunities. Make good things happen. Lose your 'wait problem'. You can sit in life and wait, and wait, and wait, for everything to be perfect. Chances are, you'll die waiting.

9. Smiling. 100% free. No talent required.

You'll notice something weird about our list? Nine? Nobody in the history of the universe does lists of nine. There aren't Nine Commandments. The Prime Minister doesn't live at number 9 Downing Street. The radio station doesn't count down the top nine records. You don't get a nine-pence piece or a nine-pound note.

So we'd like you to round us up to ten please? What's the tenth thing *that requires no talent or intelligence whatsoever?*

My #10:

And looking at our nine and your tenth, what's the life-changing takeaway (it's the same as a Chinese takeaway, but without the noodles or Egg Fu Yung. Or the barbecue ribs.)[2]

We think it might be something along the lines of remembering that talent is never enough. The best of the best don't rest on what they were born with – they dig down to get the most they can. Try our nine things and your one, and over time it will pay off.

Odd Odds

Stop taking yourself so seriously. We rather like Thomas Pyszczynski's 'Terror Management Theory', in which he argues that humans are groping to survive in a meaningless universe, destined only to die and decay. He then rubs it in by suggesting our lives have no more significance than a pineapple chunk.

Not many laughs in that! But, if he's right, we can all chill. It's the last time we're going to mention your 4000 weeks, but have you ever stopped to consider the chances of being here at all?

---

2 Or the fried rice. So, on reflection, the 'life-changer takeaway' is the exact opposite of a Chinese takeaway. Apologies for any confusion.

Some calculate the odds of you existing at 1 in 400 trillion but I'm not so sure? The stats start fairly simply with the chances of your ma meeting your pa. And then the chances of them having that first kiss, and an awkward fumble. I don't want to gross you out but in order for you to exist, your mum and dad must have had sex at least once. Hopefully, it was just a one-off, and you can now get the image out of your head. The gross bit is the number of sperm in a single shot which Google has just informed me, is about 500 million. And out of 500 million, you were made from the sperm that got to the egg first. *WooHoo!* You are already amazingly successful, the gold medallist sperm front crawler.

But, hang on, you need to factor in the chances of your grandparents meeting and your grandad doing the same 500 million sperm thing. Yes, with your grandma! It's horrific! And back through your lineage to whomever started the whole shebang. Depending on which belief system you adhere to, the chances are you'd have to trace it all the way back to Eve and Adam or us emerging, gills flapping, from the marshes. I think Ali Binazir's calculation of 1 in $10^{2,685,000}$ is more like it?

But no, it's vastly more complicated than that! We are a tiny pinprick of life on a speck of solar dust, drifting among billions of other specks. Factor in the odds of our lump of rock spinning off into the solar system after the Big Bang and then developing the right amount of gravity and water, not to mention a breathable atmosphere. And for our ball of rock to be in the Goldilocks zone of not-too-near and not-too-far from the sun that allows life to flourish at all.

If there's a one in a trillion *trillion* chance of you being here at all, owning a yacht doesn't make you great. You are already great because you've defied the odds just by existing! You're a miracle. Plus, in the face of certain death, you choose to soldier on, inching your species forward. You are going to die, and that's because you are fortunate enough to have lived.

Amen.

LIFE: THE TRUTH

'For a long time it had seemed to me that life was about to begin – real life. But there was always some obstacle in the way, something to be gotten through first, some unfinished business, time still to be served, a debt to be paid. Then life would begin. At last it dawned on me that these obstacles were my life.'

Father Alfred D. Souza (inspirational philosopher)

It's easy to snuggle underneath the duvet of excuses. Life's not fair, right? There really is too much exam pressure, lessons really are boring, teachers do nag you and your parents aren't perfect. It rains a lot too.

It's a massive advantage if you begin from a different starting point. Remember, you were made from the only successful sperm – there are 49,999,999 of your dad's tadpoles screaming that it's unfair that they didn't make it. So rather than grumbling that life's not fair, start from the realization that nobody actually ever said it was. That cuts out 95% of your low-level grumbling.

There's a lot less huffing and puffing when you realize that maths is supposed to be challenging. There are fewer histrionics when the penny drops that homework is going to keep on coming whether you want it to or not. There's a much calmer response when you understand that sometimes Wi-Fi just won't be available. There's less sighing when you understand that loads of people will have a better phone than yours.

Our advice? Chill. Rejoice that, against all odds, you're here at all. Anything else is just a bonus.

Go Love Yourself

A lightbulb is useless until it's plugged in. It needs connecting to a force. In the same vein, you need connecting to an energy force and, in case you haven't twigged, that energy force is you. You shine brightest when you're being your best self.

Glow baby, glow!

There's fitness. That's being able to run for the bus.

There's wellness. That's rarely thinking *'Shish, I feel lousy'*.

And there's super-wellness. That's having focus, clarity, imagination, creativity, energy, a quiet mind and resilience.

An ability to not just get stuff done, but know which are the right things to get done. An ability to flip that which seems a blocker into a possibility. An unstoppable love of life and delight at having landed on one of the few rocks hurtling through the Universe with oxygen, gravity and great music.

Kung Fu Panda progressed through all three. In the unlikely event you've not seen it, here's the plot spoiler: Po, a buffoon of a panda, trains to be a kung fu ninja. *Why?* To earn the Dragon Scroll which contains the secret that will enable him to fight the evil snow leopard.

With me so far?

Meantime, back at the family cafe, his father (who is a bird, not a panda – *weird!*) reveals there is no secret ingredient in the bestselling 'secret ingredient noodle' soup. The damn bird has been fooling his customers for years!

But an even bigger reveal than the fact his dad is a bird AND a pathological liar, is this ... when Po unfurls the Dragon Scroll there are no words, just a shiny reflective surface. He's looking back at himself. At first he's horrified. He was expecting to find some answers but, of course, *he is the answer*. Po is already good enough, and BOOM, he knocks spots off that evil snow leopard.

Hoorah! From unfitness, to fitness, wellness and super-wellness in 95 minutes. The village is saved, and we can do the whole thing again in Panda 2, and 3, and 4...

Who's the most important person you talk to every day? Who's the person in charge of your life? (clue, put this book down, go to the bathroom and stand in front of your very own 'secret scroll', aka the 'bathroom mirror').

That person will be there.

Indeed, the quality of the relationship with yourself determines the quality of your relationship with everyone else.

Here's a bit more science for you. Most people go their entire 4000 weeks underestimating just how important relationships are. There's a particular type of relationship, a 'secure attachment' which is especially crucial. If you're lucky enough to have developed decent bonds with your parents, psychologists would say that you've developed 'secure attachments' and you'll feel relatively safe and stable.

But what the textbooks don't ever tell you, is that the most important secure attachment you'll ever create is with yourself. Bonding with yourself is the first step. Easy to say, harder to do. Learning to love yourself, for some, is a never-ending journey. Not 'love yourself' in a sense of thinking you're better than anyone else, but 'love yourself' as in making peace with yourself and being comfortable in your own skin.

So, how do you do that? How do you become happy? *With yourself?*

Well, you might need to sit down for this bit: Breaking news: *you are NOT a cucumber.*

As well as being a bit of a relief, this is also a reminder that a cucumber seed will only ever turn into one thing. In the same way that a rose will only ever be a rose and a banana will only ever succeed in being a banana, these things are locked into one reality.

But you have a mind, which gives rise to thoughts, which gives you a lot more potential. It can't turn you into a banana, but it gives you the power to experience emotions, to think, rationalize, and imagine; all skills that elude your common or garden cucumber.

A Basic Thinking Lesson

Earlier, we splashed around in the shallow end, introducing you to some simple(ish) concepts so you could get used to them. That was in preparation for this bit. From now on, we're chucking you into the deep end.

We're confident you're ready. Hold hands, in we go ...

I'd put it to you that nobody formally taught you *how* to think. Nobody ever actually sat you down and said, *'OK mate, this is how it's done. This is a thinking lesson.'* There's no GCSE in 'thinking'. You have to think to get the answers but 'thinking' isn't taught. In fact, we cram our children full of reading, maths, science, cooking, PE, French, geography and media studies, yet the most important piece of kit – their brain – remains a mystery.

So, if nobody actually taught you to think, where did your thinking come from? Are you ready for the truth about how you learned to think? *You made it up!* You kind of learned it via osmosis. When you were tiny, your parents and grandparents had a way of thinking that you copied. And then you went to school and met 30 other kids in your class and they all had a way of thinking. You wanted to fit in so you did what they did (not knowing that they were making it up as well) and your teachers imparted a way of thinking too (they were also making it up, albeit from a slightly more experienced vantage point). But, the most crucial people in all of this were your parents. So, if you're still with me, let's probe a little deeper. Who taught your parents how to think? That's right – *their* parents. And who taught your grandparents to think? Brilliant, you've got it. *Their* parents. And they got it from *their* parents, etc. You can keep going all the way back to Adam and Eve, or monkeys (depends on your belief system).

The point is that we've ended up with quite a fixed way of thinking, passed down to us through the generations. Often it's a very defensive way of thinking. It has changed a little but the essence is exactly the same as it was 200 years ago. The world has accelerated away, and our brains are stuck in a Neanderthal loop.

THIS EXPLAINS A LOT

'My father had a profound influence on me, he was a lunatic.'

Spike Milligan (legendary British comic)

Keep an open mind on this next question, because it's a biggy. We've established that nobody actually *taught* you to think. And think of all the thinking you've done over your lifetime. All the thinking that everyone on the planet's been doing and consider this – *what if we've been doing it wrong?*

Maybe that's too strong a point. The better question might be: *what if there was a better way?*

So let's rewind to a better question: have you ever stopped to consider 'while you are busy thinking, who's the one *noticing* that you're thinking?'

Thought not!

Most of us go through our waking hours taking little notice of our thought processes. It's safe to say that how the mind goes about its business never crosses your mind. What it fears, what it says to itself, what it notices and what it doesn't notice – for the most part we go through life aware that we're *thinking* but paying minimal attention to *how* we think.

Strap yourself in for some uncomfortable stuff. There's a physical you, but there's another you *experiencing* the physical you. The flesh and blood you allows your mind to get around town. It's helpful to think of it like this; the 'you' you see in the mirror is just a means of transport. The real 'you' lives between your ears.

The real YOU lives HERE

Seatbelt fastened? That's where we're going next ...

Quantum Thinking

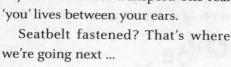

In the *deep* deep end. The only things you can change RIGHT NOW are things within. So what is this 'within' thing? If we turned you inside out and had a good look, you'd be full of slimy pink and purple stuff, some bones, a few miles of intestines and seven pints of blood. All a bit of a mess to be honest. The more interesting stuff that lies 'within' is less visible but can be of equal messiness. Your thoughts, memories and attention. Your spirit, beliefs and attitudes. These are the things that you have instant control over and these are the keys to feeling amazing.

So far, we've been laying the foundations to get you to the point of understanding that nobody ever taught you to think, hence the easiest thing is to fall in line with the rest of humanity, and think like them. While all the time we've been hinting that there is a better way.

So, step centre stage, the inside-out revolution. *Ta-da!*

We don't normally recommend sugar, but you might need to stick the kettle on and grab a custard cream before you get stuck into this next section. Before you start, remember how you learned to ride a bike? You didn't read a book about it, you just got on, your dad/grandad ran alongside for a bit and then, hey presto, off you went. A bit wobbly to start and there were a few grazed knees but then you got it. And now it's easy-peasy. You can probably let go of the handlebars?

Inside-out thinking is not information-based learning. Yes, we're going to give you an explanation but it's *insight* based. That means it requires some light bulb thinking, the *'Oh yeah, I get it now!'* moment. Just like the bike thing, once you've got it, it stays with you forever. Yes, you will still fall off sometimes but you always have the knowledge inside.

If we get up close and personal, what's inside-out all about? We've been hinting at it throughout the book. Remember the 90:10 principle from way back in Part 1? A quick reminder: you have no control over 10% of your life.

This 10% comprises of events that happen to you; you get grade A, or grade E, your homework is rock hard, or you get no homework, you are picked for the school team, or you're not picked, someone you love dies, or nobody dies, there's a massive queue at the supermarket, or there's no queue ... you cannot control the 10%. Things keep happening, but 90% of whether you have a brilliant life (or not) depends on how you *respond* to the 10%.

Taking this further, the first insight is a bit of a leap of faith – your thoughts create your feelings. So, for example, it's not your homework that's getting you down. Your homework is neutral – it means absolutely nothing, until you attach some thinking to it, *'There's so much of it and it's so boring'*, which releases a gush of feelings. You are therefore the creator of your own experience.

We class it as an insight rather than a theory. Once you just go with the flow, it can burst open the door of your potential and expose the fact that there's an awesome version of you much closer than you think. What a cunning hiding place: *inside your head!*

Let me simplify the already simple concept to this: the thoughts you make real are the source of your feelings. Yes, *your thinking is the source of your feelings.* This simple sentence turns your entire filing cabinet of lifelong learning on its head. Until now, you unquestionably imagined that external events created your feelings. The homework, or the miserable weather, that's what made you dreary. Or the heated argument with your sister, that's what made you irritated.

Or Mr Harris telling you off in geography. Or your mum nagging you. Or, let me guess, you are angry because you've got mountains of homework. You're hurt because of what someone said. Saturdays make you happy. And everyone knows that Mondays make you sad.

Unfortunately, everyone is wrong. None of this is accurate. You might want to find something to hold onto while you read this next bit: your feelings never (and I mean NEVER) come from what's happening to you. They always (and I mean ALWAYS) come from your thoughts.

Without thoughts there would be no feelings. You cannot be happy without having happy thoughts. Ditto angry, sad, miserable, fearful, jealous ...

You're not supposed to know this. Your mind goes to extraordinary lengths to convince you that the event caused you to feel in a certain way. My football team's rubbish performance made me angry. I passed my driving test which made me happy. I asked the fittest year 10 out and they said yes, which is why I'm so happy. It's 3.30 on Friday, with the whole weekend stretched out before me, which is why I'm grinning.

Erm, sorry, but nope.

Your Friday feeling is not caused by Friday, but rather how you're *thinking* about Friday. And your Monday morning downer isn't caused by anything other than how you've learned to think about Mondays.

Recognizing that it is merely your thinking, allows you to step outside of it and make a better choice, hence a calmer approach to life. Most people will sail through life reacting to external events, totally oblivious to the level of insight that this chapter has taken you.

Allow us to work through a particular situation, showing you the order of events. The *outside-in* version of you first (remember, this is how most people live their lives):

Your teacher asks you to stop talking to your bestie in maths class (and maths is boring anyway). This acts as a trigger and your emotions go off on one. The fact that you feel you're being unfairly picked on means you are immediately angry. This affects your behaviour and you sit grumpily for the rest of the lesson, doing very little work, learning zilcho, and thus reinforcing your belief that maths is a waste of time and Mr Smith is a bit of a dick. Quite frankly, an hour of your life has ebbed away and nobody has won.

Let's take the same example, but applying your new-found *inside-out* thinking.

Your teacher asks you to stop talking to your bestie in maths class (and maths is boring anyway). This acts as a trigger and your emotions go off on one. The fact that you feel you're being unfairly picked on means you are immediately angry. At this point you realize that your anger is nothing to do with your teacher but 100% to do with your thinking. This opens up a few choices for you. You can either change your thinking (*'Err, sorry Sir. But I'm struggling with question 8. When you get a min can you come and explain it in a different way?'*) or wait a nano-second for a better thought to emerge.

A productive thought for me is ALWAYS *'How would the best version of me act in this situation?'*

Technically, the *outside-in* version will operate in this four-step process:

1. Trigger (teacher asking you to stop talking)
2. Feeling (instant feeling of being picked on)
3. Behaviour (tune out for the rest of the lesson)
4. Outcome (an hour of your life ebbs away, pointlessly. You've ruined your teacher's day too btw.)

The *inside-out* model, adds a step:

1. Trigger (teacher asking you to stop talking)
2. THINKING (how would the best version of me react?)
3. Feeling (calm and relaxed)
4. Behaviour (*'Sorry Sir, I'll crack on'*)
5. Outcome (a productive hour of maths. Your teacher gets home and punches the air.)

It's a game-changer. But it's also a very slippery concept. The inside-out model means you need to get your head around the fact that all events are neutral. So there is no good or bad weather, until you apply thinking. There are no good or bad subjects, until you apply thinking. Homework is neutral, until you apply thinking. The big hurdle is to understand that Mondays and Fridays are totally equal, they're both worth a seventh of your life, and Mondays only become bad when you apply thinking to them. (Yes, we understand how challenging this last one is, because it goes against everything you see around you.)

Its slipperiness comes from the speed of thought. Often, you don't have time to rethink your thinking. It's like trying to stop a sudden sneeze. There's snot shooting across the room before you knew it was coming. '*Soz, Miss Alexander. It's dangling on your cardigan.*'

Thinking is even faster than snot globules. The trick with *inside-out* thinking is to understand your entire experience of life is coming to you via your thinking.

Always. Forever. No exceptions.

Understanding this stuff doesn't make you immune from trauma and unhappiness. It doesn't prevent disappointment. Sometimes bad stuff happens and life doesn't work out. The power comes in realizing you have choices about what thoughts you make real next. This is the 'gap of infinite possibilities' that we spoke about earlier. You have choice, and that gives you power over the situation.

The great news is the more we pause and think '*How would the best me deal with the situation*?' the better and easier life becomes.

You don't have to wait for your circumstances to change, and that's crucial.

There's Magic in Your Genes

JUST SAYIN'

It's very simple to make things difficult and very difficult to make things simple.

At ninja level, *inside-out* is about less effort. You don't even have to change your thinking, merely to realize that any bad feelings you experience are created by thinking, and another thought will be along in a few seconds. Let that angry one pass and, hey presto, I'm going jump aboard this positive one instead.

Activity: The weight of the world

Grab a water bottle. A full one. Hold it at arm's length. Easy, right?

Keep holding it. And keep holding it some more. And more. *Mooooooore.*

Until it becomes not so easy.

In fact, it's not long before the very lightweight water

bottle starts to feel a whole lot heavier. Your arm aches. If you stick at it, your arm will eventually shake and give way. It's the same with negative thoughts. Holding onto old thinking, rethinking negative experiences, nasty comments or events just weighs you down. Once you realize it is all just thinking you can let stuff go. *Phew!* All of a sudden life seems a lot lighter.

So, here goes, the entire reason for writing this book, to lure you this far and blow your mind with something that your author tag-team doesn't quite understand – epigenetics. It's a brand-new strand of science, hideously complex and unfathomable to everyone except a few white-coated academics with extra-large foreheads.

In the same way that Harry Potter can be summed up as '*Boy wizard goes off to boarding school, finds his true self, fights baddies and saves the world*', here's our summary of epigenetics ...

Starting with the very basics. Our genetic code is inherited from our parents so certain aspects such as eye colour, hair colour, body shape and height are fixed. So, your genetic 'code' shapes your body and it gives a starting point for your mind *but it needs activating.*

It boils down to this: having healthy and positive thoughts is more than a nice feeling. These thoughts will trigger certain genes into action, thus re-wiring your brain and changing your life for the better. So, it's true that your genes are fixed. But epigenetics explains that the sequencing of your genes (which ones are switched on and off) is down to your mind.

Therefore, positive emotions (remember, these can only ever come from one place, your *thinking*) are not just 'nice to have' or something you should reserve for Friday evening. Training yourself to be a 2%er will create more happy/positive thoughts, which create uplifting emotions, which alter which genes are switched on and off.

Why are we telling you this?

Because it links with our earlier point that you might be trapped inside the stereotypical teenage hamster wheel, grumbling that *'It's not fair'*, and you'd be bang on correct. It's not. Remember our point from earlier? Nobody ever said it was.

Often people are suffering and creating stress for themselves by thinking *'Why is this happening to me?'*

You've heard of fake news. This is fake stress.

Exams happen to everyone. So does being dumped. Ditto, having a massive row with your bestie. And guess what, very few people will reach the ripe old age of 16 without being trolled online.

Suffering therefore is not because life is difficult but because people are expecting life to be easy. It isn't. *Get over it!* It's a plot twist. That's part of the fun!

But the much bigger point is that being stuck in the hamster grumble wheel will be re-wiring your brain towards negativity. And my goodness, it's easy to get stuck there!

PLOT TWIST

When something goes wrong in your life just yell 'plot twist' and move on.

Activity: Extracting the good from the bad

List three significant negative events in your life. What positive message can be taken from these events? (e.g. *'It taught me to be strong'*, *'It taught me that I can survive'*)

1

2

3

How can these lessons improve your future?

Who's the happiest person you know? Looking at them ... what can you learn about happiness?

Who's the least happy person you know? Looking at them, what can you learn about happiness?

What are the three wisest happiness lessons you've learned, so far?

Struggle is good for you. Hard graft makes you stronger. Let me prove it to you. A couple of years ago I visited my local primary school, where the children proudly showed me their incubator, filled with yellow fluffy chicks. They were beyond cute (the chicks, not the kids. They were savages.).

The children had traced the development of the eggs right the way through to hatching. *'Except,'* said one of the eight-year-old girls, *'one of them didn't make it'.*

'Oh dear,' I gulped. *'Didn't it hatch?'*

'It tried,' she said, rolling her eyes and pointing at one of the boys. *'He decided to help it hatch. He was so excited when he saw the egg cracking that he took a penknife and cut a hole in the egg so the baby chick could escape.'*

'And it did,' said the boy defending his position.

'And it died,' she reminded him. *'Mr Bromwich said it was because the chick needs to struggle. All that pecking and flapping to get out strengthens its wings. He says it's sometimes good to struggle.'*

Nice lesson Mr B. Sometimes the act of struggling makes us stronger.

Mind-ful or Mindful?

Careering to the end of this final part, that you may or may not have understood, there's still one thing missing.

The power of NOW.

We're told to live in the moment but this is a really hard thing to do. Which moment? There are so many of them!

Well actually, no. There is only ever one moment. It's called 'now' and it's right here. It always has been and it always will be. The truth is that the present moment is here. The question is, where are you?

Here's where it gets tricky. We get that you're a young person and that various forms of social media and technology are part and parcel of life. To suggest you should cease would be, quite frankly, ridiculous and unfair. All we ask is that you read this final section in exactly the same way that you read all the other sections, with a wide-open mind.

It's a half-decent guess that, more often than not, your moments will be spent scrolling or texting. With a tablet or smartphone at your side, the question arises, can social networks promote meaningful human relationships, or are they fuelling superficial ones? The stats tend to suggest the latter. Obviously, social networks allow you to keep in touch with a wide range of friends and acquaintances, plus a whole gaggle of people you don't know.

And for the record, sending pictures of your private parts really doesn't make any long-term sense. No, not even if everyone else is doing it.

In a very short space of time, there's been the rise of the 'e-personality', something that amplifies the self-centred side of human beings. There's a lot of hating out there. It's easy to hate and to join in with conversations that, if they were face-to-face, you wouldn't enter into. I'm assuming that if I met you in the street, you'd be a nice person and a decent human being? If I encountered you online, would you be the same? The basic rule is to be nice on social media too. Remember, it's called 'social' media, not 'anti-social' media, so please use it as such.

You've got to the end of the book so here's the punch line; social media is not your purpose. You were not put on this earth to spend nine hours a day scrolling, texting and gaming. While everyone around you is eating their precious time doing exactly that, you can be getting on with achieving your secret long-term ambitions – your Huge Unbelievably Great Goal will be taking shape.

As for the power of now? You're built for the reality of the present moment. When the future arrives, IT will be the present moment. The reality you're built for is here and now.

One of the questions might be, why are we born not knowing this? Why are we fooled into thinking the world is *outside-in*? My answer is that we *are* born knowing this, but we forget!

Your average toddler lives in the 'now'.

SOMETHING TO AVOID...

'Most people tiptoe through life, hoping to make it safely to death.'

Earl Nightingale (the so-called 'Dean of Personal Development')

Here's a plot spoiler – you might be putting your happiness in the wrong time zone. Life is nothing but a series of nows. If I leave the terrifying notion of how many 'nows' have passed you by because you've been too busy focusing on the past or the future, the point of mindfulness is that there is no 'past' or 'future' as such. Everything you ever experience is experienced through the lens of now. So all the fabulous stuff you've done in the past can only be remembered as you are now. And your future can only be imagined from the point of now. The past and present can only be comprehended in this moment of thought. They don't exist anywhere else.

Gulp!

If you delve a bit further, to be embarrassed about something you did yesterday you have to remember yesterday NOW and create bad feelings in the present (you might have to re-read that a couple of times before it sinks in). Your bad feelings aren't stored anywhere. There's not some bottomless well of shame or sorrow that you can tap into or, conversely, an unbridled spring of joy. It's all accessible through thought and absolutely nowhere else. *'Now where did I put that depressed feeling? Oh yes, last year when my boyfriend dumped me ...'* and off you go, one thought and you've jumped into a self-created reservoir of rage.

The incident happened four months ago and one thought can take you back there. But you can only get back there through the wormhole of NOW.

Which brings us to our final question: what have the Greeks ever done for us?

Apart from yoghurt, marathons, democracy and inventing the Olympics. Oh, and Mykonos.

Read on ...

I once met a man who said he didn't have time to be happy, so he was going to schedule it in for *'about November time'* (our discussion was in February!).

There are lots of versions of time and we all have our personal favourites – mine are 'dinner time', 'bed time', 'quiet time', 'me-time' and 'down-time'. My all-time #1 is 'family-time'.

The Greeks on the other hand? They have two versions of time. *Chronos* is the time that you and I think of, the ticking *Countdown* clock variety. The time of day, the stage of life you're at – the point being that it's limited – when it's gone it's gone.

The Greeks also have *Kairos*, a more personal sense of time. A realization that the time is right.

Chronos tells us that time is limited and *Kairos* that the time is right. Our entire book has been pointing to this very moment. Here's a truth that hurts the author team. We're old! Like, over 40? This is no longer our time.

You're young. Your life is stretching out ahead of you. For you, it's *'Kairos* time'.

The time is right.

This is your time.

It's ticking.

Please make the most of it.

About the team

Dr Andy Cope is a teacher, best-selling author and learning junkie. He's got the coolest job in the world, studying happiness and wellbeing and then sharing the results with who ever will listen. He's worked with Lego, IKEA, Microsoft, UEFA and other super duper cool companies. He's written 40 books, including the world famous 'Spy Dog' series and a host of happiness books aimed at adults and children. Andy runs workshops for teachers and young people.

Twitter @beingbrilliant

Instagram artofbrilliance

Facebook Art of Brilliance

Jason Todd is a mover and shaker whose achievements include floating a company on the stock market (£22 million) and setting up and selling two other successful businesses. He's also worked on building sites, delivered coal and been a fireman. Interesting facts: Jase has climbed the highest mountain in Europe (Elbrus 5642 metres), and flown into the stratosphere in a Russian fighter jet. Jase now works as a trainer, delivering the messages in this book for adults, teenagers and parents. This is his first book and he's proper excited!

Twitter @jasontoddtalks

Darrell Woodman? He's the quiet(ish) one. He's been going about the daily business of delivering workshops that change people's lives for about ten years. Loads of laughs, no big words or nonsense. He absolutely loves it. Daz has worked with household names such as Nationwide, National Lottery and the NHS. He also delivers keynotes and workshops for teachers and young people. This is Daz's second book. [He says to tell you he doesn't do all that social media nonsense.]

Amy Bradley drew the pictures and front cover. We love working with Ames cos she's young, talented, creative and female. She keeps us in check. Ames has a fab little studio in Staffordshire where she illustrates a whole range of books, posters, teeshirts and greetings cards. She's super excited to have a CBBC series in the pipeline.
Twitter @amy_brad1
Instagram amysillos

That just leaves Andy Whittaker. All you need to know about Andy W is that he's 'special' in almost every way. He provides the team with a lot of words but they don't always make sense so we have to delete them, or re-write them into actual sentences. Andy wasn't a huge success at school, at least not if you measure him academically. But he's proof that personality and humour are vital ingredients in the modern world. He's not weird, he's 'limited edition'.

Andy's a very funny man. His actual job is to deliver keynote speeches and workshops in business and schools.
Twitter @artofbrillandyw

Check us out at www.artofbrilliance.co.uk or at our schools website www.brilliant.school

HAPPINESS

Your route map to inner joy

Andy Cope, with Andy Whittaker and Shonette Bason-Wood

There's a saying that happiness is a journey, so we're taking you on one – a magical mystery tour – on which we encounter dead-ends, sharp bends and plenty of lessons on the way to 'happiness central'.

Happiness is the definitive route map that shows you not only where, but also how. It teaches you to harness your thoughts, memories, ideas and attention to embrace 'now', experience more joy and live a truly flourishing life.

This book is a wake-up call to stop skimming the surface of life, take charge of your attitude and set your path for enlightenment.

Buckle up. You can expect peril, thrills, science and extreme laughter along the way.

The average life-span is just 4,000 weeks. Quit waiting – now is the time to start embracing life.

Paperback ISBN: 978 1 473 65103 6
eISBN: 978 1 473 65104 3
www.hodder.co.uk

THE LITTLE BOOK OF EMOTIONAL INTELLIGENCE

How to Flourish in a Crazy World

Andy Cope and Amy Bradley

Are you caught in a busyness trap, living life on fast-forward, working too hard and counting down the days to your next holiday?

It's time to stop kicking happiness into the long grass. This funny and profound book is about intelligent living – uncovering why you feel the way you do and showing how to transform your thinking so you can live a full colour, high-definition, surround-sound life.

This sideways look at a world which is at times overwhelming will help you:

- Unpick limiting beliefs
- Be your best self
- Tilt at happiness
- Discover how to live a flourishing life.

Paperback ISBN: 978 1 473 63635 4
eISBN: 978 1 473 63636 1
www.hodder.co.uk

LEADERSHIP

The Multiplier Effect

Andy Cope, with Mike Martin and Jonathan Peach

This is a leadership book for people who need to bridge the chasm between theory and the real world. Employment has moved on, rapidly and profoundly, and the new world has a different set of challenges and rules.

9–5 has become 24/7. Life is full-on, relentless and exhausting. The pressures are immense and it's easy to end up careering from one crisis to another, and existing from one holiday to the next.

In short, the leader's job has morphed into an ongoing challenge of squeezing more from less. To do it well requires new ideas, new skills and – most importantly – a new attitude. Your job is not to inspire people – it is to BE inspired.

This fascinating, humorous and insightful book shows how everything follows from there.

Hardback ISBN: 978 1 473 67945 0
eISBN: 978 1 473 67946 7
www.hodder.co.uk